The Future of Think Tanks and Policy Advice in the United States

James McGann

The Future of Think Tanks and Policy Advice in the United States

palgrave
macmillan

James McGann
University of Pennsylvania
Philadelphia, PA, USA

ISBN 978-3-030-60385-4   ISBN 978-3-030-60386-1   (eBook)
https://doi.org/10.1007/978-3-030-60386-1

Cover illustration: © Melisa Hasan

This Palgrave Macmillan imprint is published by the registered company Springer Nature Switzerland AG
The registered company address is: Gewerbestrasse 11, 6330 Cham, Switzerland

Acknowledgement

I would like to thank my very dedicated and able research interns from the University of Pennsylvania and the 70 interns from colleges and universities from across the US and around the world for their assistance collecting data and conducting background research for this book. I would like to especially thank Varsha Shankar who provided invaluable help with the editing of the early drafts of the manuscript and shepherding the book and the flock of 64 authors from start to finish. I also want to thank the 64 CEOs of think tanks that provided thought provoking and forward looking essays for this book. Additionally I want to thank the Lauder family and especially Ambassador Ronald S. Lauder and Martin Haas, director of the Lauder Institute, for their support and encouragement of my research. Finally, I want to thank Maya, my daughter, and Emily, my wife, for their patience and understanding for the nights and weekends I spent away from them working on this book.

CONTENTS

LIST OF FIGURES

Introduction and Background

James McGann

Abstract James McGann, Director of the Think Tanks and Civil Societies Program, Lauder Institute for Management and International Studies, University of Pennsylvania in Philadelphia, PA, explores the Future of Think Tanks and Policy Advice in the United States.

Keywords Civil Society · Policy advice · Policy analysis · Research Institutions · Think tanks · Transparency

THINKING ABOUT THE FUTURE OF THINK TANKS: CATALYSTS FOR IDEAS, INNOVATION, AND ACTION

The changes we continue to witness in the twenty-first century are proving to be far more revolutionary, dynamic, and impactful than any before. Far from what many believed to be the post-Cold War "End of History," we are undergoing seismic shifts in technology, culture, and geopolitics. These developments reach across national borders into every

J. McGann (✉)
Think Tanks and Civil Societies Program, Lauder Institute for Management and International Studies, University of Pennsylvania, Philadelphia, PA, USA

© The Author(s) 2021   1
J. McGann, *The Future of Think Tanks and Policy Advice
in the United States*, https://doi.org/10.1007/978-3-030-60386-1_1

aspect of society. Think tanks, a core sector of public and international affairs, are no exception.

Whether it is changing their goals, sources of funding, or use of technology, think tanks are a part of this global evolution. The purpose of this text is to explore the changing landscape that think tanks find themselves in. The future of think tanks poses many challenges to the sector, but with these obstacles come opportunities for the savviest competitors to distinguish themselves and leave profound impacts on civil society. To further an understanding of these challenges, it is vital to hear the perspectives and ideas of those currently in the midst of this changing landscape. For this purpose, presidents from top think tanks within the United States have contributed essays detailing their own experiences and expectations for their institutions and for the think tank community in a broader sense. These writings give a glimpse into a myriad of different perspectives surrounding the evolution of think tanks, and have the unique characteristic of being written by those who not only study the subject, but are actively engaged in shaping its future. This allows the reader to better understand not only the directions that think tanks may take as they move into the future, but also the rationals or beliefs guiding these new directions.

These essays will not only describe this changing landscape, but also illustrate the importance of think tanks in creating a lively and useful policy landscape within the United States. These institutions provide ideas for policymakers that can help create solutions for some of the most challenging issues facing the country at any given moment. Without the work of think tanks, the debate surrounding policy proposals within the United States would lose an essential aspect of factual fuel, drastically hurting the nation's ability to improve existing policy and create effective new programs and laws. Think tanks also have the capability to address long-term and complex issues, such as the Fourth Industrial Revolution, changing economic structures, and a rebalancing of global power that persist not only within the United States, but across the globe. As national governments have become incapacitated by gridlock and polarization, think tanks have an enormous opportunity and responsibility to address the forthcoming challenges. These institutions will have to adapt to a changing political landscape, but their importance to the policy process must remain constant.

In order to remain relevant in a world that increasingly disdains established knowledge and expertise, think tanks have begun taking on new roles in society. The primary impetus for these shifts has been the increasing difficulty to reach policymakers, who were once think tanks' exclusive audience. The dawn of the digital revolution has created an information ecosystem where the creation of and access to policy recommendations has never been easier. While this progress has benefited society by furthering democratization, it has also had the adverse effect of straining governments' limited bandwidth.

In response to increased competition over government access, in some instances, think tanks have started acting as advocacy groups. Once again, technology has been a key factor in making this possible by changing the way think tanks both communicate and publish research. Wider access to the internet, and specifically social media, has allowed think tank research to become more accessible to the general public. However, social media has also posed a challenge to think tanks by limiting media consumption to the fastest and easiest forms possible. This has forced some think tanks to focus less on traditional methods of output, such as: books or scholarly articles, and focus instead on quick, easily accessible work to satiate the new fast-paced information landscape. These conflicting priorities can either be solved by hiring multimedia experts or training current researchers, both of which require additional funding that is increasingly difficult to receive.

However, with this increase in the production of quick and easy-to-read forms of media, there is also a concern that think tanks may begin to take the role of news agencies instead of institutions whose primary focus is policy research. In order to maintain relevance in the eyes of the public, some think tanks have tried to generate commentary on current issues or events. This can distract institutions from the goal of generating policy solutions to long-term issues, which often permeate beyond the scope of day-to-day news coverage. While the news media undoubtedly has an important role in any democratic society, this is a role that has traditionally been separate from the role of independent policy research institutions. If think tanks begin to blur the lines between these separations, it may create a vacuum in the space of policy research. The research, proposals, and ideas that think tanks generate are vital to the creation of successful policy within the United States, and it is important that think tanks retain the capacity to continue to generate solutions to issues that extend beyond the confines of what the national spotlight happens to be centered on during any specific day.

Think tanks have also begun to increasingly use technology in their research. The ability to accumulate enormous amounts of big data can create sources of information that were previously unheard of in the research community. This data can be extremely useful for a think tank's ability to accumulate enormous amounts of information within a short time span, but the challenge now shifts to creating effective methods to sort through this data. This again will force many think tanks to adapt their practices to fit into an increasingly technology-oriented world, as it demands that they control a tight command over modern data analytics and understanding.

Another major challenge facing the think tank sector is global political polarization. Some think tanks are responding to these shifts by taking on explicit partisan viewpoints and only conducting research that will support or strengthen their agenda. Many of these institutions also have a separate advocacy partner institution, often in the form of a Political Action Committee (PAC), which takes part in explicit political actions. The purpose of these relationships is to enable think tanks to directly influence political parties and the structure of governments. This system is perpetuated by perverse incentives that enable partisan government officials to leave office and enter into these institutions, which further polarizes the think tank landscape and concentrates ideologies into biased echo chambers that lack objectivity.

Sources of funding have also drastically changed in recent decades in ways that exacerbate the issue of polarization and may discredit the think tank industry. The principal driver of these shifts has been the systemic decrease of large institutional grants in favor of smaller, project-specific-donations. Many prominent think tanks have begun to try to diversify sources of funding, which will hopefully decrease the outsized influence of individual donors.

Relating to the issue of funding has been the recent proliferation of think tanks. As the number of think tanks has increased, it has allowed for certain institutions to develop expertise in one specific issue. This phenomenon has in turn allowed for smaller institutions to amass considerable influence on issues pertaining to their area of expertise, creating a more diversified field of policy ideas. Conversely, this has also created more competition for funding, as donors now have a plethora of options to choose from when deciding where to donate their money. This makes it even more important for think tanks to be able to distinguish themselves in this diverse field.

As think tanks approach the coming age, it is increasingly important to develop a mutual code to ensure the quality of their research. This may include increased transparency, which can help consumers of information understand who or what, is funding an institution. This may also protect think tanks from external criticism based solely upon their sources of funding, helping to protect the position and respect that think tanks hold in the policy world. In addition, these can ensure a level of integrity in the work that thinks tanks are completing to promote accurate and well-informed research within the country's top policy institutions. In an increasingly polarized environment, it is vital that the work that think tanks do does not value ideological beliefs over objective facts.

Think tanks play a vital role in the development of effective public policy. In the global revolution that we are now living in, think tanks must continue to be an advocate for and utilizer of facts and reason. Many of the changes that the world faces will be long-lasting and omnipresent, and it is the duty of think tanks to prepare the world for this new age. As the ways in which this role is conducted changes, the fundamental purpose remains the same, to provide useful policy analysis. This book draws upon the experiences and insights of thought leaders in the think tank community to not only help examine and prepare for upcoming challenges but also to demonstrate the continued importance of think tanks in society.

Literature Review

The Fifth Estate: Think Tanks, Policy Advice, and Governance in the United States

James McGann

Abstract James McGann, Director of the Think Tanks and Civil Societies Program, Lauder Institute for Management and International Studies, University of Pennsylvania in Philadelphia, PA, explores Think Tanks, Policy Advice, and Governance in the United States.

Keywords Advocacy tanks · Policy advice · Policy experts · Policy research organization · Revolving door · Think tanks · Transparency · University-affiliated

This study was launched to examine the changes that are affecting think tanks and policy advice in the United States; as well as to examine how think tanks are adapting to the rapidly changing policy environment in which they now operate. Think tanks can be defined as public policy research, analysis, and engagement institutions that generate policy-oriented reports on domestic and international issues, which enable policymakers and the public to make informed decisions about public policy issues (McGann 2007). Think tanks are typically regarded as having six

J. McGann (✉)
Think Tanks and Civil Societies Program, Lauder Institute for Management and International Studies, University of Pennsylvania, Philadelphia, PA, USA

© The Author(s) 2021
J. McGann, *The Future of Think Tanks and Policy Advice in the United States*, https://doi.org/10.1007/978-3-030-60386-1_2

9

main functions. These include carrying out basic research on public policy, providing advice on immediate policy concerns, evaluating government programs, interpreting policy and current events for different media, facilitating the exchange of ideas, and to supply the government with policy experts and provide a place for those leaving the government to continue their work. While think tanks are a diverse group of institutions, there are six major types of think tanks: university-affiliated, political party-affiliated, academica-oriented, government-affiliated, contract-oriented and advocacy/policy entrepreneurs (McGann 1995). Today, the term "think tank" is a bit of a misnomer since these organizations do more than just "think"—many policy research organizations describe themselves as "think and do tanks." This study will examine the changing nature and role of think tanks in a more deeply polarized nation and how think tanks are adapting to a society increasingly centered around technology. Further, it will examine the changing methods employed by think tanks to achieve their goals, and how these goals have drastically shifted in recent decades. In addition, this report will predict how current changes will continue to affect think tanks in the future. In The Fifth Estate, Dr. James McGann illustrates how policymakers have come to value the independent analysis and advice provided by think tanks and why it has become one of the defining characteristics of the American political system (McGann 2016). He also defines and describes the "revolving door," a characteristic of think tanks deeply embedded in American politics and culture (McGann 2016).

In recent decades, think tanks in the United States have both expanded and, in some cases, changed, the goals they seek to accomplish. Think tanks grew out of the intellectual movements of the nineteenth century (McGann 1995). These institutions were dedicated to providing objective and nonpartisan policy advice to the government (Abelson 2006). The first major think tanks were established in the early twentieth century when a "majority of their intellectual and financial resources were devoted to preparing studies on a wide range of policy issues" (Abelson 2000: 217). They largely attempted to stay "detached from the political process because of their commitment to preserve their intellectual and institutional independence and not influence policy decisions directly" (Ahmad 2008: 532).

However, in the second half of the twentieth century, think tanks began to enter into a more politicized era. The emergence of liberalism in the 1960s helped to initiate this partisanship and led to a conservative reaction in the 1970s (Ricci 1993). They began to introduce "for the first time marketing techniques" to make their research more prevalent (Ahmad 2008: 532). Newer think tanks that engage in this work are often referred to as "advocacy tanks" (Ahmad 2008). These new think tanks are blatantly partisan and tailor research to fit their ideological predispositions (Ahmad 2008). Indeed, the "ideological revolution" of the 1970s, which facilitated the entrance of conservative think tanks into the sphere of ideas, saw the rise of the polarization of think tanks (Katz 2009: 7). The increase in party polarization apparent in US politics in recent decades has created a need for legislators to find supportive explanations for their policy ideas (Bertelli and Wegner 2009). Think tanks have been able to fill this role (Bertelli and Wegner 2009). However, as politics have become trapped in inaction due to partisanship, think tanks have an opportunity to rise above the bickering and establish themselves as developers of research-based solutions (McGann 1995). The proliferation of think tanks has also led to increased competition between different institutions, creating more specialized think tanks (Stone 2013). These smaller and more specialized think tanks can "wield influence out of proportion to their small size" due to their level of focus and expertise on a particular area or issue (Wiarda 2015: 519). Society has become saturated with public policy organizations, meaning that in order to stay relevant, think tanks must become efficient, accountable, and innovative (McGann 1995). In addition, these think tanks came into existence along partisan lines (McGann 1995).

There has also been a shift of some think tanks toward advocacy instead of pure research—classified as "advocacy tanks" (Weaver 1989: 566). The new advocacy-based think tanks "realise that in order to shape the policymaking environment, they must convey their ideas to the electorate in a straightforward and lucid manner" (Abelson 2006: 224). Many scholars believe that this new focus has weakened the integrity of these new think tanks (Abelson 2006: 220). This focus on direct advocacy also provides an avenue for large donors to take part in the policy process, as advocacy-based think tanks pressure "decision-makers to implement policies compatible with their ideological beliefs and those shared by their generous benefactors" (Abelson 2000: 220). In order to help protect their integrity, many think tanks have shown "interest in a collection of policies and procedures for think tanks that can be put in place to ensure the quality, independence, and integrity (QII) of their research" (McGann 2015: 9).

However, certain think tanks base their funding model off of the idea that they will base their projects around the wishes of certain clients. These think tanks often utilize scholars to create objective reports that are commissioned by certain clients, with this often driving funding for the institution (McGann 2015). These reports are not made for the general public, and may often be viewed only by the institution that commissioned them itself. This differs from the more traditional model of a think tank as a "university without students" that typically has a long-term and objective viewpoint (Weaver 1989: 563). Funding for these institutions is usually supported by corporations, foundations, and individual donors (Orlans 1972).

Some scholars have attempted to define think tanks by where they receive funding. According to these schools of thought, "the objectivity, direction, and influence of a think tank" can all be influenced by the source and nature of the funds that a think tank receives (Durst and Thurber 1989: 14). As think tanks have begun to face more competition within a larger marketplace for ideas, some think tanks may have to increasingly bend to the will of donors in order to stay financially stable (Stone 2000). All think tanks face the same challenge: how to achieve and sustain their independence, so they can speak "truth to power" or simply bring knowledge, evidence, and expertise to bear on the policy-making process. In order to maintain integrity, "transparency in funding" is becoming increasingly important for the purposes of "maintaining the trust of the public and protecting the independence of research" (McGann 2015: 9). However, even with these difficulties, think tanks "are relatively cost-effective compared to universities and other research organizations" (Weidenbaum 2010: 47).

Many of the changes that think tanks face as they adapt to new styles of organization are facets of the Fourth Industrial Revolution, which is affecting all aspects of the globe (McGann 2018). There are four key trends that are changing the global landscape, these being: the power of social media, big data, and artificial intelligence to disrupt; an increasing rate of technological change; global information interdependence; and an increasing velocity of the flow of policy and information (McGann 2018). These trends not only put the availability of information and data at an unprecedented level, but have also allowed dramatic increases in the ability to share and manipulate this information (McGann 2018). This information revolution has created widespread political and societal disruptions across the globe, and think tanks are not exempt from this (McGann 2018). This disruption is only intensified by growing insecurity about the economy, Post-World War II global order, physical security, national identity, and lack of sufficient answers to these challenges (McGann 2018). In the face of growing anxiety about the state of the world, think tanks must fill a void that has been left empty by partisan governments locked in gridlock and societies anxious about uncertainties (McGann 2018). This role is to be able to provide answers and recommendations that are founded upon facts and evidence to the immense problems facing all people. This may be increasingly difficult to do in a society where it is increasingly easy to spread disinformation or regard expertise with disdain, but, beyond these challenges, there are many opportunities for think tanks to seize during this historic moment (McGann 2019). These opportunities include the ability (or necessity) to solve some of the most complex problems the world has ever faced, change how think tanks are organized, and create new channels of interaction with the public (McGann 2019). In addition, they must operate with vigor, accountability, and speed in order to attain success in this changing landscape (McGann 2019). If think tanks take these opportunities, they can evolve into multidimensional, global institutions (McGann 2019).

One changing aspect of think tanks in this historic age is their new methods of interacting with the general public. This is becoming an increasingly important opportunity, as we are witnessing a public that is increasingly insecure and distrustful of institutionalized knowledge (McGann 2019). Think tanks can serve as the connection between the policymakers and the public (McGann 2019). Many think tanks have begun to track "output," or how often they take part in something that may generate publicity (Weidenbaum 2010: 135). These may include "the number of publications it issues, the frequency that staff members appear on national television, and the numerous citations of its activity in the print media" (Weidenbaum 2010: 135). While these measurements show think tanks are developing an emphasis on public communication, there are drawbacks. The pure numbers of publications may look impressive, but "the number of books written by a group's scholars does not distinguish between those widely distributed volumes that have a national impact and the more specialized works that appeal to a more limited scholarly or technical audience" (Weidenbaum 2010: 135). In addition, "citations in the Congressional Record and in congressional hearings and committee reports may be more indicative of policy impact than the sheer number of materials published and distributed" (Weidenbaum 2010: 135).

Despite the fact that "measuring tangible impact is difficult at best, setting specific, measurable goals for various outputs is the best place to start" (McGann 2015: 14). These may include tactics such as using "web analytics to measure dwell time on target project web pages, the reach of their infographics, and number of plays on their videos" (McGann 2015: 14). Using strategies such as these microsites and new types of digital communication can result in "a measurable impact on policymaking" (McGann 2015: 14). Many larger think tanks also have "full-time publicists, editors, media advisors, and public relations sections" who help facilitate the sharing of research and ideas out of think tanks (Wiarda 2015: 521).

However, these new innovations, and their impact on how think tanks interact with people are not the only technologies affecting think tanks. Think tanks can now utilize "interactive websites, infographics, podcasts, Twitter aggregator tools, big data visualization, videos, embedded microsites, special challenges, and even Soundcloud" (McGann 2015: 10). These new forms of communication allow think tanks to disseminate research to much larger audiences, and across much larger geographical areas than previously possible. Another use of technology will be the use of big data in conducting research (McGann 2015). Some scholars say that it "is very effective at showing correlation (although not causation) and that it can be harvested much more quickly than traditional data" (McGann 2015: 11). This can help think tanks conduct research projects faster and on a larger scale than previously possible.

In conclusion, it has become apparent that think tanks are in the process of changing on multiple fronts, and have already changed dramatically from their early twentieth-century beginnings. On one front, partisanship and political engagement of think tanks on all sides of the political spectrum have increased, leading to a more "active" generation of think tanks. In addition, think tanks have begun to find new sources of funding, and as a result, are learning how to navigate through potential conflicts of interest. It is now important for think tanks to balance the need for funding with the integrity of their research, an issue that will continue to develop in future years. Finally, think tanks need to adapt to a more technological world, learning how to use new technologies in both their communications with policymakers and the public and using innovative techniques in their own research. While all these changes do present a shift in the work of think tanks, think tanks remain vital to the policymaking process and will continue to be vital in this new era.

REFERENCES

INTRODUCTION AND LITERATURE REVIEW

Abelson, Donald E. 2000. Do Think Tanks Matter? Opportunities, Constraints and Incentives for Think Tanks in Canada and the United States. *Global Society* 14 (2): 213–236.

Abelson, Donald E. 2006. *A Capitol Idea: Think Tanks and U.S. Foreign Policy*. Montreal: McGill-Queen's University Press.

Bertelli, A., and J. Wenger. 2009. Demanding Information: Think Tanks and the US Congress. *British Journal of Political Science* 39 (2): 225–242.

Ahmad, Mahmood. 2008. US Think Tanks and the Politics of Expertise: Role, Value and Impact. *The Political Quarterly* 79 (4): 529–555.

Durst, S., and J. Thurber. 1989. Studying Washington Think Tanks: In Search of Definitions and Data. Paper presented at the Annual Meeting of the American Political Science Association, 31 August–3 September 1989, Atlanta, USA.

Katz, Michael L. 2009. American Think Tanks: Their Influence Is on the Rise. *Carnegie Reporter* 5 (2): 7.

McGann, 2007. *Think Tanks and Policy Advice in the United States: Academics, Advisors and Advocates*. Routledge: New York.

McGann, James G. 1995. *The Competition for Dollars, Scholars, and Influence in the Public Policy Research Industry*. Lanham: University Press of America.

McGann, James G. 2015. *Global Think Tank Innovations Summit Report: The Think Tank of the Future Is Here Today*. Philadelphia: Think Tanks and Civil Societies Program, University of Pennsylvania.

McGann, James G. 9 February 2016. 2015 Global Go to Think Tank Index Report. Scholarly Commons, University of Pennsylvania. Accessed November 7, 2018. https://repository.upenn.edu/think_tanks/10/.

McGann, James G. 2018. *Think Tanks: A Bridge Over Troubled Waters and Turbulent Times*. Philadelphia: Think Tanks and Civil Societies Program, University of Pennsylvania.

McGann, James G. 2019. *2019 European Think Tanks Summit*. Philadelphia: Think Tanks and Civil Societies Program, University of Pennsylvania.

Orlans, Harold. 1972. *The Nonprofit Research Institute: Its Operation, Origins, Problems, and Prospects*. New York: McGraw-Hill.

Ricci, David M. 1993. *The Transformation of American Politics: The New Washington and the Rise of Think Tanks*. New Haven: Yale University Press.

Stone, Diane. 2000. Think Tanks Transnationalization and Non-Profit Analysis, Advice, and Advocacy. *Global Society* 14 (2): 153–172.

Stone, D. 2013. *Capturing the Political Imagination: Think Tanks and the Policy Process*. London: Routledge.

Weaver, Kent R. 1989. The Changing World of Think Tanks. *Political Science and Politics* 22 (3): 563–578.

Weidenbaum, M. 2010. Measuring the Influence of Think Tanks. *Social Sciences and Public Policy* 47: 134–137.

Wiarda, H.J. 2015. Think Tanks and Foreign Policy in a Globalized World: New Ideas, New "Tanks," New Directions. *International Journal* 70 (4): 517–525.

Former President's Historical Perspective

Building the Belfer Center for Science and International Affairs

Graham Allison

Abstract Graham Allison, Former Director of the Belfer Center for Science and International Affairs at Harvard University explores the history, evolution and future of think tanks and policy advice in the United States.

Keywords Policy advice · Policy analysis · Research centers · Research institutions · Think tanks · University-affiliated

The former President of Harvard University has labeled me a "serial entrepreneurial institution builder." As "Founding Dean" of Harvard's John F. Kennedy School of Government, I had the opportunity to create a vision, develop a strategy for pursuing it, recruit a faculty, and build a campus. After a dozen years in that job, I took a year's leave of absence, expecting to return to Harvard to engage in the research and teaching that had attracted me to the University in the first place. After a stint as Assistant Secretary of Defense in the first term of the Clinton Administration, I did return to teach and write about the public policy challenges that have been the focus of most of my professional life. Nuclear weapons

G. Allison (✉)
Harvard Kennedy School, Cambridge, MA, USA

J. McGann, *The Future of Think Tanks and Policy Advice in the United States*, https://doi.org/10.1007/978-3-030-60386-1_3

and the risk of nuclear war had captured my imagination and stirred my soul since the Cuban Missile Crisis in fall of 1962. As a young graduate of Harvard College who had just arrived at Oxford, I lived through what historians agree was the most dangerous time in recorded history, when the world teetered on the brink of nuclear catastrophe.

But as I have discovered repeatedly in life, events intervened. Two colleagues from the initial phase of the undertaking who remained good friends, Joe Nye (who had become Dean of the Kennedy School) and Al Carnesale (who had become Provost of the university), invited me to what they said would be a "long lunch." Little did I imagine that they were to explain to me the travails of the Center for Science and International Affairs, which had been the first research center established during my deanship to focus on central challenges of international security—including nuclear risks. Their message: this Center was in deep trouble. As a result of the new leadership's efforts to take the Center in a different direction, the founding director, Paul Doty, had drafted a letter to the Ford Foundation urging them to demand that the gift it had made to endow the Center be returned. Long story short, over the next several months, Joe and Al persuaded me that my duty was to become Director of CSIA, right the ship, and set it on course—after which I could go back to my professional life. As fate had it, that effort took two decades.

In the process of agreeing to become Director, Carnesale and Nye suggested that we engage Robert Belfer, a successful oil entrepreneur who had been a major donor and supporter of the Kennedy School during my Deanship. Over those years, I had become personal friends with Robert and his family. Those conversations concluded with Carnesale's proposal that the Center be "refounded;" that Belfer provides a major gift to reendow the original CSIA; that the renewed Center be renamed the Belfer Center for Science and International Affairs; and that I serve as Director with a commitment to do my best to build a world-class independent research center focused on international security. To quote the contract from my proposal and Belfer's pledge: "the goal will be to make the Belfer Center for Science and International Affairs the leading independent center in the world advancing policy-relevant knowledge about the most important challenges to American national security in the next quarter-century and beyond."

At the conclusion of my tenure as Director of BCSIA, and at the urging of the Belfer family and the Kennedy School Dean, I provided an account of where our effort in renewing the Belfer Center had begun, and where

I was leaving the enterprise for my successors, Ash Carter and Eric Rosenbach, whom we had recruited to become Co-Directors for the next phase of the enterprise. That foreword to my final Annual Report on the Belfer Center provides, in effect, a case study of one strand in the evolution of the think tank industry.

When I became Dean of what was to become the modern Kennedy School of Government, a fellow Dean told me: "the best donor is a dead donor." I never believed it. As Dean, I thought of donors as investors: staking their money, time, and energy together with university staff, scholars, and students to support initiatives we all believed in. I often remind faculty and administrators that they have opportunities to pursue worthy projects only because of the generosity of donors/investors. The Center's leadership is obligated to manage these ventures to earn outstanding returns. And I have been honored to have the Belfer family as the anchor investor in the venture.

Among the one-liners I most treasure from my years leading the School and the Center was Bob Belfer's declaration that, over a lifetime of business and philanthropy, his gift to create the Belfer Center yielded the "highest returns of any investment he had ever made." He demonstrated that this was not simply rhetoric when he stepped up with a substantial reinvestment to make it possible to bring the next generation of leadership to the Center.

One of the most severe tests of leadership in any enterprise is succession. This was one of the issues Belfer and I prioritized when we developed the strategy for transforming the Center. Anyone who underestimates the critical importance of this factor has learned a painful lesson watching GE. In 1999, legendary CEO Jack Welch prepared to retire after fifteen years at the helm of one of America's leading companies. When asked about his legacy, he said "My success will be determined by how well my successor grows the company in the next 20 years." One can only wonder what Welch thought near the end of his life. Tragically, a storied company that grew 40-fold under his leadership has under his successor shrunk to half its value—a shell of its former self.

On the succession test, only time will tell. Nonetheless, I am confident that we passed. Thanks to an extraordinary triple-team effort by Robert Belfer, me, and a new Dean, Doug Elmendorf, in selecting and recruiting former Secretary of Defense Ash Carter and his Chief of Staff Eric Rosenbach to succeed me, we secured two proven stars of the next two generations. They are now leading the Belfer Center to new heights.

(I have had the good fortune to know Ash since 1983, when I appointed him as an Assistant Professor at HKS, and Eric since he arrived at the School as an MPP student in 2002.)

The following highlights 12 points from my two decades of "refounding" BCSIA. But before outlining them, I should make a broader point about organizational leadership that may help those charged with founding or revitalizing their own research institutions. It's common today to hear scholars and academics complain that we live in a "post-truth" environment that devalues expertise. I sympathize with this critique, but I also contend it is hardly a new phenomenon.

Strains of anti-intellectualism and anti-elitism have recurred regularly in American history. As founding dean, just as I was working to build up the nascent John F. Kennedy School of Government, a former B-list actor turned politician was telling Americans not to trust experts and public officials. In his inaugural address in 1981, President Ronald Reagan went even further, declaring: "Government is not the solution to our problem; government is the problem."

Reagan's proposition was, in effect, the very antipode of the Kennedy School's mission. Surely, this new ethos from Washington would demoralize students, depress donors, and suppress scholarship. Far from it. The early Reagan years were some of the young Kennedy School's strongest years of growth. We did it not by changing course but by tacking into Reagan's headwinds. We knew that rhetorical attacks on elite institutions like Harvard could not erase the continuous demand for competence. And we knew that savvy relationship building, far more than resistance, would yield opportunities to shape the administration's work in positive directions. Most observers were shocked when less than six months after his inauguration, thanks to extraordinary efforts by a former Kennedy School lecturer, Richard Darman, the Director of the School's Institute of Politics, Jonathan Moore, and me, the administration asked the School to conduct special classes for new subcabinet appointees. Indeed, members of his team cohosted these with me and provided the Roosevelt room in the White House as the venue. Later, in an effort to lead by example, I personally joined the Reagan administration on a part-time basis as Special Adviser to Reagan's Secretary of Defense Caspar Weinberger.

My advice to the next generation of institution builders is simple enough: don't despair. From the founding of the Republic until today, most Americans have believed that government was at best a "necessary evil." Americans have always been fearful that a federal government strong enough to perform the "necessary" duties would be so strong that it would abuse their freedoms—like the tyrant King George did. But as the Constitution summarizes the essence of the matter: government is necessary to "establish justice, insure domestic tranquility, provide for the common defense, promote the general welfare, and secure the blessing of peace and prosperity to us and our posterity." A one-liner that I found effective in responding to the skepticism of some of the participants in the program we cohosted for the Reagan Administration, and with skeptical potential donors thereafter, asked: If you don't want competence in our government, how are you going to defend the nation from foreign foes, ensure law, order, and justice to protect citizens from criminals or threats to public health, provide a currency for exchange, and monetary and fiscal policy to promote a growing economy? In sum, hostility to your work should get your juices flowing and stretch your imagination to demonstrate why competing in government is something we cannot survive without. Be open to strange bedfellows. And always remember: it's not about you. It's about putting forward people and ideas that can help build a better society here at home and a safer more prosperous world.

1. Where we began: 1996. Appendix is my January 1996 proposal to transform CSIA into the new Belfer Center. I always try to begin with what I call the Nietzsche question: What were we trying to do? (A plaque in my office reminds me daily of Nietzsche's one-liner: "The most common form of human stupidity is forgetting what one is trying to do.")

    As that proposal states: "the goal will be to make the Belfer Center for Science and International Affairs the leading independent center in the world advancing policy-relevant knowledge about the most important challenges to American national security in the next quarter century and beyond." We recognized that this was audacious; we discussed at length the risk that this could appear presumptuous. But those are the words we settled on.

    Belfer noted at the time that they echoed our earlier experience in building the Kennedy School. When I had become Dean of the Kennedy School in 1977, my first speech to the Visiting Committee outlined a dream of a professional School of Government that would take its place alongside Harvard's major professional schools of Business, Law, and Medicine. As I put it, we aspired to build a new School of Government that would "serve society's demands for excellence in governance in many of the ways Harvard's Schools of Medicine, Law, and Business have come to meet analogous demands in their respective private professions." But recognizing that this might strike some as delusional, I recalled Lord Acton's advice to would-be institution builders. He recommended that they begin with a "remote and ideal objective" that "captivates the imagination by its splendor and simplicity and thereby evokes an effort that could not be commanded by lesser and more proximate goals."

Both in the case of the School in 1977 and CSIA in 1996, our stated objectives certainly passed the Acton test. CSIA had, of course, been the first research Center established under my deanship, reflecting my own interests and convictions that security is the prerequisite for everything else. Its founding Director, Paul Doty, had set high standards for policy-relevant, science and technology-based work, but the Center had wandered off course. As a reminder of where we stood at that point, note that the proposal aspires to double the core of international security heavyweights from the starting 4; to restructure the Center; and then to move out smartly in executing a strategy that is defined in some detail.

2. Harvard Kennedy School's Belfer Center for Science and International Affairs is No 1. The Center's Director of Global Communications and Strategy, Josh Burek, produced the graphic below (Fig. 1) charting performance over the past two decades "by the numbers." These include budget, endowment, core leadership, faculty, senior fellows, pre- and post-doctoral fellows, students, etc. But for a Center whose one-phrase summary of our benchmark is to be "simply the best," one number matters most. The fact that thought leaders and practitioners in international security increasingly refer to the Center as "No. 1" is significant. We have been happy to see that judgment reflected in the University of Pennsylvania Global Go-To Think Tank Index, which has consistently named BCSIA as the "No 1 university-affiliated think tank" in the world.

3. Clarifying the mission. One of the first steps in developing the strategy for building the new Center was to clarify its mission. As

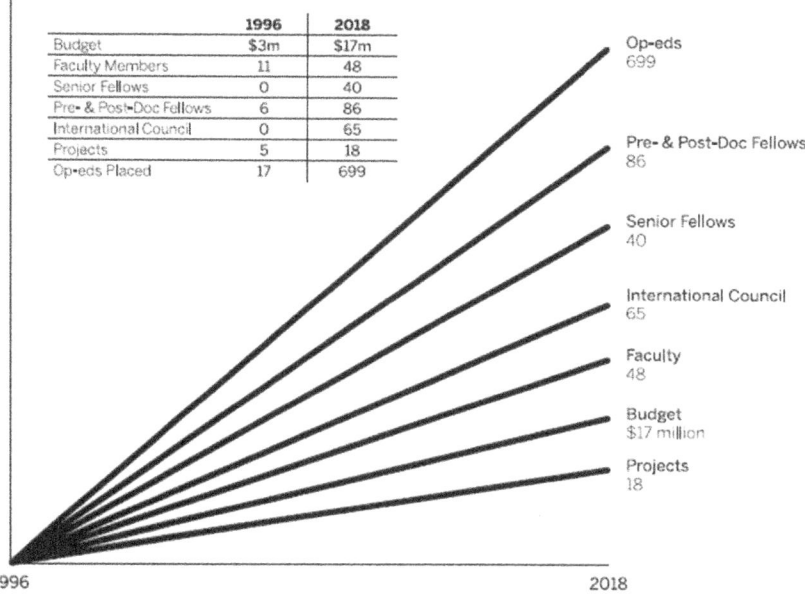

	1996	2018
Budget	$3m	$17m
Faculty Members	11	48
Senior Fellows	0	40
Pre- & Post-Doc Fellows	6	86
International Council	0	65
Projects	5	18
Op-eds Placed	17	699

Op-eds
699

Pre- & Post-Doc Fellows
86

Senior Fellows
40

International Council
65

Faculty
48

Budget
$17 million

Projects
18

1996   2018

Fig. 1   Key metrics for Harvard Kennedy School's Belfer Center for Science and International Affairs, 1996–2018

I stated, repeated, and sought to get the leadership of the Center to feel in their bones, the Center has a dual mission to:

(a) Provide leadership in advancing policy-relevant knowledge about the most important challenges of international security and other critical issues where science, technology, environmental policy, and international affairs intersect.

(b) Prepare future generations of leadership for these arenas.

Every phrase in the mission statement was carefully chosen. Thus, for example, in the annual review of the agenda pursued by each of the major programs and projects, we asked: Is this one of the "most important challenges?" Is this enterprise actually "advancing policy-relevant knowledge?" And by "policy-relevant," we pressed those leading research projects not just to demonstrate that their work was "policy related"—since almost any academic work can, with a stretch, pass that test. The question is whether the research is "engaging" policymakers in ways that actually have impact for good.

This has meant establishing thick relations between analysts at the Center and those on the front line of policymaking. It has meant building a community on campus that combines the best of scholarship in the university, on the one hand, with the best of practice in policymaking, on the other. To this end, we have made a special effort to engage individuals who stand firmly on two legs: one foot planted solidly in the world of independent, objective analysis that meets the test of scholarship in a leading university; the other in the realities of the practice of policymaking.

Unlike other research centers at the School, or analogous centers at other universities, most of the leadership at the Belfer Center has lived in both worlds. While a professor who goes to Washington to become Undersecretary, then Deputy Secretary and then Secretary of Defense before returning to become Director of the Center is extraordinary, most of our professors and research leaders have held significant positions in government that inform their scholarship, including Meghan O'Sullivan (who was Deputy National Security Adviser), Nick Burns (who was Undersecretary of State), John Holdren (who served as the Science Adviser to the President), or Joe Nye (who was Chairman of the National Intelligence Council). Visitors from think tanks or other universities repeatedly comment on the Center's unparalleled critical mass of faculty, research leadership, and former senior government and military officials who are all part of a single community that is pursuing a common effort to build a more secure, peaceful world.

4. People: recruiting and engaging the best.

Research centers are the sum of its individual members. Recruiting, engaging, and nurturing a community in which there is a sense of common purpose are major challenges for the leadership of a research center.

This has always been among my highest priorities, and we have been fortunate. Our faculty and research leadership of each of the core programs are the envy of any other research center in the world. These include Steve Walt and Steve Miller for International Security policy; John Holdren, Venky Narayanamurti, Dan Schrag, and now a co-directorship between Holdren and Schrag of Science,

Technology, and Public Policy; Bill Clark and Henry Lee in Energy and Natural Resources, including the outstanding work of Meghan O'Sullivan and her Geopolitics of Energy Project; and finally Nick Burns, who has been our trailblazer in establishing a major new pillar focused on diplomacy.

I regularly compare the leadership of each of our programs and projects with those of our competitors. And while one can't say it without seeming to boast, it is a simple fact that there are few other research centers that would not be significantly strengthened by attracting even one of our stars. And I can think of very few stars at other research centers we have been unable to attract when we thought they could add significant value to our enterprise.

The commitment to attract and engage "the best" reaches beyond the leadership of each of the programs to the faculty who are associated with the Center (many of whom are members of other departments at Harvard or MIT), the Senior Fellows, the core staff, and the pre- and post-doctoral fellows and students who are all part of the larger family.

Among recently retired military leaders, our Senior Fellows Joe Dunford, Vincent Brooks, and Sandy Winnefeld are more than outstanding. In the world of intelligence, former Director of National Intelligence Jim Clapper and former House Intelligence Committee Chairman Mike Rogers are again each not just good, but the best. In the world of diplomacy and international organizations, Laura Holgate, Doug Lute, Samantha Power, Susan Rice, Wendy Sherman, and Bob Zoellick are unparalleled. On issues of science and public policy, Holdren, Venky, and Schrag are renowned figures who would at any other research center elevate it to the first ranks. Among historians who are prepared to explore how we can make history more relevant for policymakers in developing a new subfield of Applied History, Niall Ferguson, Fred Logevall, and Arne Westad are each stars.

I am particularly gratified that our efforts have succeeded in recruiting back to the Belfer Center not just Ash Carter and Eric Rosenbach, but John Holdren (the longest-ever serving science advisor to the president) to codirect the Science, Technology, and Public Policy Program; Samantha Power (former Ambassador to the United Nations); and at least a piece of Ernie Moniz (former

Secretary of Energy) who will be leading a study for a joint project between MIT and the Belfer Center.

5. Addressing the "most important challenges in international security." Since its origins, the Center has recognized that nuclear weapons pose the gravest threat to international security. While we can be thankful that we have seen seven decades since Hiroshima without another use of nuclear weapons in war, the United States and Russia continue to maintain nuclear arsenals that if used in a full-scale war could extinguish all human life. The Harvard-MIT community, including Paul Doty, Tom Schelling, and Henry Kissinger, were part of the first generation of thought leadership about how to manage international affairs in a world that lived under this nuclear shadow. Doty's purpose in launching the original project on science and international affairs was to build on that foundation to foster future generations to address these challenges. Over the decades, the Center has continued making significant contributions in this arena, including the Avoiding Nuclear War Project of the 1980s that Carnesale, Nye, and I codirected; providing the intellectual foundations for the Nunn- Lugar Cooperative Threat Reduction Program in the 1990s; sounding the alarm about nuclear terrorism after 9/11; identifying the threats posed by Iran's and North Korea's nuclear programs and ways to combat them over the past decade; and the ongoing work of the Managing the Atom project, chaired by Matt Bunn.

Other mega-threats, including biological weapons, cyber, and even mega-terrorism are also important strands in the Center's agenda. Juliette Kayyem (former Assistant Secretary of Homeland Security) is building our Homeland Security Project. Michael Sulmeyer, reinforced by Eric Rosenbach and others, laid the foundations for fundamental contributions to better understand cyber threats and ways of coping with them. John Holdren, Dan Schrag, Henry Lee, Bill Clark, Robert Stavins, and others have helped us understand how unchecked greenhouse gas emissions could create a climate in which no one would want to live, and have been leaders in identifying policies that will allow us to satisfy energy demands without spoiling the environment.

The nations that pose the most serious challenges to American national security today and for the generations ahead are China and Russia. On the China front, the Center's China Working Group, co-chaired by Larry Summers and I, has brought together the best Harvard China experts, including Rod MacFarquhar, Dwight Perkins, and Ezra Vogel, with colleagues including Joe Nye to try to better understand the impact of the rise of China on the United States and the international order. My recent national best-seller, *Destined for War: Can America and China Escape Thucydides's Trap?* is a signature product of that effort. On the Russia front, thanks to Kevin Ryan and Rolf Mowatt-Larssen, the Elbe group (which includes retired four-star military and intelligence officers from the United States and Russia) has become the best—but at this point, sadly the only—high-level Track II conversation between Americans and Russians in an era in which this relationship has become so toxic that it raises real risks of the parties stumbling into a conflict neither wants and each knows could be catastrophic for both. A new project and website dedicated to objective facts, Russia Matters, has quickly made the Center one of the go-to places for analysis of these issues.

6. Advancing the frontiers of science, technology, and public policy. Again, since the Center's origins, science and technology have been fundamental to its mission. That was the reason founding Director Paul Doty chose what seemed at the time an odd name for the enterprise when he called it "Science and International Affairs." This reflected his recognition that science and technology are major transformers of both the challenges we face in international affairs (from nuclear weapons and cyber, to a potentially uninhabitable climate), and of the actions we can take to address these challenges.

Most public policy analysis—including the dominant form of analysis taught and practiced at the Kennedy School—is essentially applied micro-economics. It accepts current technical parameters of a challenge and analyzes options within that box to find the most cost-effective option. In contrast, science and technology-based analysis sees today's technical parameters as variables that are evolving as science and technology advance. Indeed, it asks how investments in R&D or new regulations can advance desired changes that move these parameters to enlarge the box. Thus, while economists' analyses are typically static, searching for the best option within current parameters, analyses driven by S&T are dynamic.

An example may make these generalities more concrete. Robert Stavins's ground-breaking research on "cap-and-trade" shows how rather than setting a single limit on all greenhouse gas emitters, an alternative that establishes a limit on the total amount of emissions but then allows entities to trade vouchers will achieve the same objective at lower costs. Those for whom reducing emissions is expensive can buy vouchers from emitters who can reduce them at lower costs.

Belfer Center science and technology analysts offer two further big ideas on climate change: (1) changing the conventional correlation between economic development and pollution, for example, by investing in low-carbon sources of energy like solar, wind, biofuel, and other new technologies; (2) redefining the problem, for example, by targeting the negative consequences of greenhouse gas emissions rather than the emissions themselves. For example, through targeted introduction of phosphates into the atmosphere, geo-engineering could mitigate harmful rays from the sun. From public investments in basic science to the education and training of scientists and engineers, to regulatory policies that inhibit, or alternatively enable, advances in science and technology, S & T analysts insist that choices governments make can shape both the challenge and the solutions.

7. Diplomacy. Nick Burns sometimes teases others at the Center by noting that there are ways for nations to resolve their differences without bombing one another. He has taken the lead in creating a new Diplomacy and International Politics program within the Center to demonstrate that fact. His Secretary of States Project with Harvard's Robert Mnookin and James Sebenius has interviewed all living Secretaries of State in order to capture their key lessons in statecraft. In conjunction with Harvard's Business and Law Schools, the Diplomacy Project also selects a "great negotiator" annually, brings them to campus for discussion with faculty and students, and produces a case for classroom exercises. The Diplomacy Project also covers our Middle East Initiative. MEI has ensured that the Center and the School have a lively representation from across the region and are active participants in the efforts to deal with its complexities, including the Israeli-Palestinian conflict.

8. Women leaders in international security. Recognizing that women have historically been underrepresented in the study and practice of

international security, and most especially on issues of hard power, the Center has attempted to seize this opportunity to encourage and empower talented women. In reaching out to students, pre- and post-docs, and practitioners, we are proud that we have made modest progress. Our alumni who served in major roles in government have included Michèle Flournoy (Under Secretary of Defense for Policy), Liz Sherwood-Randall (Deputy Secretary of Energy), and Laura Holgate (the US Ambassador to the International Atomic Energy Agency). We have also been fortunate to be able to attract an outstanding group of veterans of recent government service including faculty members Meghan O'Sullivan, Samantha Power, and Juliette Kayyem, as well as our Senior Fellows Wendy Sherman, Lori Robinson, Lisa Monaco, Victoria Nuland, Paula Dobriansky, Laura Holgate, Farah Pandith, Debora Plunkett, Liz Sherwood-Randall, and Susan Rice.

9. Intelligence Program. Thanks to Tom Kaplan's generosity, we have created the Recanati-Kaplan Fellows program for outstanding analysts from the United States and other friendly intelligence agencies. There is no analogous program in the world. CIA, DNI, NSA, Mossad, and others recommend rising stars who spend a year at the Center in individually tailored study programs that help prepare them for leadership in their agencies. They enroll in courses (I typically have 3 in my course on national security challenges). They participate in daily Center seminars and study groups with the National Security Fellows, pre- and post-docs, MPP, and MPA degree students. They take part in seminars led by the program's Executive Director. They meet with current and former intelligence chiefs when they visit the Center. This program not only gets rave reviews from the agencies who send fellows, but has also enhanced the rest of the Belfer community's appreciation of intelligence as a key instrument in international security.

10. Defense Program. The Belfer Center has become the recognized "home" for active duty military officers and vets at Harvard. Our library is the locus for their weekly "Common Defense" seminar. They are active participants in the Director's lunches and seminars that occur daily. The National Security Fellows are 25 fast-track military officers who come to Harvard as an alternative to going to the National War College. They attend courses, seminars, participate in working groups, and enrich the entire community as we try

to understand both the critical role for, and the limits of, military force.

11. Best Analysis. At the end of the Cold War when the Soviet Union disappeared, the Center played a key role in identifying the risks that "loose nukes" would soon find their way to international arms bazaars. We proposed several actions to meet this threat, including what became Nunn-Lugar Cooperative Threat Reduction programs that Ash Carter and I had the good fortune to help implement as Assistant Secretaries of Defense in the Clinton Administration. About the risks of nuclear terrorism and ways to combat it, the Center took the lead. As Iran's nuclear program advanced from years to only months away from its first nuclear bomb, a collective effort at the Center targeted the issue and, as the leader of a competitor put it, "owned" the issue. While these efforts included numerous classified and private contributions, public articles, reports, and books convey the essence of our contributions. On all of these issues, Congress has a key role and its discussions and debates are reflected in public testimony. We were proud, therefore, that both Republican and Democratic legislators looked to the Belfer Center for the best analysis of the issues and a non-partisan assessment of the pros and cons of various ways to address them. This produced some memorable moments, for example, when Chairman Corker of the Senate Foreign Relations Committee thought that there had been a mistake when he discovered that both the expert chosen by the Republicans and the one chosen by the Democrats came from the same Belfer Center.

12. Communications. In 1996, the Center had one assistant for communication. His main job was to handle the occasional press inquiry and help Center scholars place op-eds. There was no website. Today, the Center gets more interview requests—and publishes more op-eds—in a single day than we did in a month back in 1996.

On a dollar for dollar basis, we believe that no research center in the world competes more effectively in the marketplace of ideas than the Belfer Center. Consider the number of Center books that have become instant classics. From Joe Nye's work on soft power and Niall Ferguson's definitive biography of Kissinger to my own treatment of nuclear terrorism and US–China relations, Center experts have authored some of this century's most influential works of global affairs. The Center's sponsored journal, *International Security*, has been ranked among the top three journals in international affairs in each of the past ten years. But while we aspire to be timeless, we understand that we also have to be timely: In a recent year, our expert community published a stunning 699 op-eds. These were not placed in niche outlets but in the world's leading media. Indeed, the Center published 108 op-eds during this period in the nation's three most competitive newspapers: *The New York Times, The Wall Street Journal*, and *The Washington Post*.

Op-eds, of course, are supplemental to our signature academic output: reports and papers. We published 52 of these over the past year, and none sat on a shelf collecting dust. The Center long ago recognized that even elite institutions have to "push" their work to key audiences. We do so actively. From arranging briefings with members of Congress to e-blasts that convey key findings to Capitol Hill staffers, we promote our work assertively. For example, in the wake of the 2016 presidential election, we held a major national security conference for Washington's leading journalists and Capitol Hill staff. Topics included Russia, China, Muslim immigration, nuclear threats, and cybersecurity. Our faculty and senior fellows thickened relations with elite media—including *The Wall Street Journal, The New York Times, The Financial Times*, and *The Atlantic*—and deepened their value to journalists as go-to resources for insight and analysis about critical foreign policy challenges facing this administration.

BelferCenter.org has become a leading source of relevant research for policymakers, government officials, academics, students, and the media. We are particularly pleased to have launched (on budget) a completely redesigned website this past year. Optimized on both the front and back ends, the new site integrates several of our "satellite" sites, which means more of our scholarship on critical issues—such as the Iran nuclear deal— is accessible in one place. From JFK Jr. Forums to our quarterly newsletter, the Center makes sure that policymakers, academics, government officials, and journalists know about our signature work.

Communications have evolved rapidly since 1996, and we are evolving rapidly with it. Today, we promote the Center's work on multiple digital platforms, including Twitter, LinkedIn, and

Facebook. We have our own multimedia production team, so we can create and share video highlights, and record podcasts. Over a million people have watched videos on the Center's YouTube channel. The Belfer Center hosts nearly 400 events each year, more than one per school day. To return to Nietzsche, all of these communications channels exist for one reason: to help the Center in its mission to make a more secure, peaceful world.

In conclusion, leading the "refounding" of what is now BCSIA was a great opportunity. I am proud of what was achieved during my tenure. And for readers weighing the pros and cons of institutional leadership versus their own personal scholarship, I hope this case will be helpful. As a teacher who helps awaken a mind or an author who advances knowledge about something that matters takes a measure of satisfaction in having made a contribution beyond themselves, leaders who build institutions that enable many researchers and many teachers to do so, can also be grateful for their opportunity.

Nonetheless, as I handed the baton to my successors, Carter and Rosenbach, I recalled Winston Churchill's oft-quoted response to a constituent who stood up in the auditorium at a political rally to berate him for drinking so much champagne. She charged that if all the alcohol he had personally consumed were poured into the auditorium, it would fill the space from the floor to the top of her head. Churchill began by looking at the floor of the room, gradually raising his gaze to look her squarely in the eyes, and then looked slowly up to the ceiling before responding: so much accomplished, so much remaining to be done.

Think Tanks: Where We've Been and Where We're Going

Ed Feulner

Abstract Ed Feulner, Founder and Former President of The Heritage Foundation in Washington, DC, explores the history, evolution and future of think tanks and policy advice in the United States.

Keywords Policy advice · Think tanks

In 1973, The Heritage Foundation was a small, unimportant and ignored organization," the *New Republic* wrote in 1985. "Twelve years after, it is the most important think tank in the nation's capital."

A decade later, the *Wall Street Journal* affirmed this judgement: "No policy shop has more clout than the conservative Heritage Foundation."

More recently, a *Politico* reporter referred to Heritage as "the crown jewel of the conservative movement," echoing the words of a *Guardian* columnist who noted in 2017 that Heritage staffers "wield unparalleled influence" upon the Trump administration.

I don't share these quotes to boast, although I'm certainly proud of our accomplishments. I'm including them because they underscore just how far we've come in a relatively short period of time. A look back at

E. Feulner (✉)
The Heritage Foundation, Washington, DC, USA

© The Author(s) 2021   35
J. McGann, *The Future of Think Tanks and Policy Advice
in the United States*, https://doi.org/10.1007/978-3-030-60386-1_4

what we did to create and nurture Heritage over the decades offers some important lessons for think tanks struggling today to make their mark and influence public policy.

The *New Republic* was right, after all. In 1973, the year of Heritage's founding, we were indeed a "small, unimportant and ignored organization." The question is, how did we change that in only a few years—to the point where President Reagan, shortly after taking office in 1981, was giving his staff copies of our first "Mandate for Leadership" report and telling them to implement its recommendations?

The short answer is that we redefined what it means to be a think tank. It required a new philosophy and a fresh outlook—one that we were determined to develop and implement.

Think tanks had been around for quite a while before Heritage came along. The Brookings Institution, for example, was founded in 1916 and was already well-known on Capitol Hill. The Hoover Institution at Stanford University celebrated its centennial in 2019. The American Enterprise Institute traced its beginnings back to the Great Depression.

They and other think tanks had been producing studies for years before Heritage opened its doors. Policymakers also had long been turning to various universities and colleges for intellectual ammunition. So why did we create Heritage?

Two reasons. For one, most of the think tanks and universities then producing studies came from a distinctly liberal perspective. (More conservative groups are around today, but the ideological spectrum is still slanted to the Left.) With the center and the Left so well-represented, there was plenty of room for an organization that would approach policy debates from an unapologetically conservative view.

The Left had a finely tuned policymaking machine. The Right had nothing to match it.

Think tank leaders of today should take note of this if they hope to amplify their voice and make a difference. We identified a need that wasn't being met, then worked to fill that need.

As Capitol Hill staffers who worked for conservative policymakers in Washington, DC, we knew firsthand how they lacked the resources of their liberal colleagues. They needed a well-funded, well-oiled policy shop that could give them the intellectual ammunition required to take principled stands on the issues of the day. Today's think tank leaders striving for success should ask themselves: What needs aren't being met, and what can I do to meet them?

Our second reason for launching Heritage was that we wanted to create a think tank that would move in a quicker and more nimble fashion, producing studies that would be relevant today and tomorrow, not yesterday.

As hard as it may be to believe now, that was not the prevailing attitude among think tanks in the early 1970s. Consider how one think tank at the time handled a study on a now-forgotten issue: funding for something known as the supersonic transport plane, or SST.

As historian Lee Edwards later wrote, "Most conservatives felt that the funds for the SST should come from the private sector rather than the public sector, although some favored continuing the program at taxpayer expense so as to maintain U.S. technological superiority over the Soviets, who had begun SST test flights that year. But they lacked the authoritative analysis that could guide them in a debate."

I was working as the senior staff assistant for the late Rep. Philip Crane of Illinois at that time, and having regular breakfast meetings with a friend of mine, Paul Weyrich, who was press secretary for Sen. Gordon Allot of Colorado. Shortly after the vote, Paul showed me a monograph produced by a right-of-center think tank: a study with an in-depth analysis of the SST issue. Paul contacted the think tank's president. "Great study," he said. "Why didn't we get it sooner?" The response: "We didn't want to affect the outcome of the vote."

This reply struck us as completely counterproductive. What's the point of producing a study when it's too late to do any good?

Our think tank, unlike earlier ones, was dedicated from day one to producing studies ahead of any votes—in plenty of time to influence the debate and make a difference on public policy decisions. The time to issue a research paper on agricultural policy, for example, is when Congress is about to take up the latest farm bill. The time to discuss the need for more school choice is when lawmakers are due to consider a federal education bill. And so on.

If today's think tank leaders want to score victories, it's imperative to strike when the policy iron is hot. Research papers, public events, and other policy efforts must be timed to ensure they're useful to the target audience. Producing such materials too far ahead of time, or just about anytime afterwards, is usually pointless. They simply won't have any measurable impact. Paying attention to the debate—indeed, talking to insiders who can give you a clue as to what is coming up and when—often means the difference between success and failure for a think tank.

Being timely, however, is just one part of the equation. From the outset, we were also determined to give policymakers the information they needed as concisely as possible.

Studies that go on and on for dozens of pages have their uses, but for busy policymakers, they might as well not exist. We instituted what we call "the briefcase test" to keep many of our reports short (no more than 8–10 pages). They focused on the facts as quickly as possible, enabling policymakers to slip them in a briefcase and read them swiftly as they shuttle from meeting to meeting.

We learned that we could make a lot of headway with people when you make it easy for them to digest the information you're providing them. Think tank leaders need to develop the habit of scrutinizing all of their public materials and making sure that they're as clear and as "to the point" as possible.

There's no need to tell a reader everything you know about a topic. Readers can always be referred elsewhere for more information. Tell them only what they need to know to make your case, then stop.

It also pays to make every effort to get that information into their hands. Effective promotion is absolutely key. That's something Heritage has always been very proactive about, from the pre-Internet days when Heritage staffers hand-delivered our studies to congressional offices, to today, when outreach is more technologically advanced but no less personal.

We've always placed a heavy emphasis on marketing our studies, and as the quotes I cited at the beginning of this article indicate, it has paid big dividends. The clout that they speak of is the result of not only producing reliable studies, but of disseminating them with speed and efficiency.

A study can be concise and timely, but if you don't get it into people's hands, you're wasting your time. This is even truer today than it was in 1973. Nowadays, the demands on people's attention have grown in a seemingly exponential fashion. We have access to more information than ever, but as the saying goes, it can be like drinking out of a firehose. Knowing the key players in your audience—and getting them what they need, when they need it—is vital.

And I'm not just talking about products, but also people. Our policy analysts and research fellows don't simply write. They appear on TV and radio. They testify before Congressional committees. They speak to editorial boards. And they work with new members of Congress to get them up to speed on the most pressing issues of the day.

Another guiding principle for Heritage from day one: We don't buy credibility, we build it. Other think tanks make a point of hiring people who are already recognized experts, but our philosophy is more like that of a "Moneyball" scout in baseball: We go out and find the most promising young talent possible, then give them the training and guidance they need to become leading lights in their field.

We also have always made a point of harnessing all of our human resources. We don't rely only on a couple of superstars to carry the load. "People are policy" has been our motto from the start. Our first "Mandate for Leadership," for example, was written by more than two dozen groups totaling more than 200 staffers and volunteers, working on different sections to create a comprehensive product that no one person could have pulled together in so short a time.

It all comes down to how you run your business—and I can assure you, running a think tank as a business was a new idea in 1973. Good ideas are the bedrock of any think tank, but to be truly effective, you need a budget, and you need a plan. You also need to be willing to tweak both as circumstances change, and give yourself room to grow.

That's just as true today as it was then. Think tank leaders need to stand out not by duplicating what others are doing, but by identifying current needs and finding ways to fill them. There's no point offering another version of what policymakers can get elsewhere. Success comes when any business leader—whether he or she runs a think tank, a Fortune 500 company, or a small business—identifies an unfilled or poorly filled need, and works to fill it.

And that's not just good advice for new businesses, but for established ones as well. We at Heritage take the need to continue innovating and excelling very seriously. We're constantly measuring our effectiveness and making whatever adjustments seem necessary. Every business leader who wants to get on top and stay there should do likewise.

In the early 1980s, the Soviet newspaper *Pravda* admitted that "in a matter of just 10 years, The Heritage Foundation has covered a mind-boggling distance." *Pravda* isn't around anymore to chart our progress after 45 years (which is no coincidence). But if it were, I'd tell them, "You ain't seen nothing yet."

Looking Back at the Stimson Center's Role in the Early Twenty-First Century

Ellen Laipson

Abstract Ellen Laipson, Distinguished Fellow and President Emeritus at the Stimson Center, Washington, DC, explores the history, evolution and future of think tanks and policy advice in the United States.

Keywords Civil society · Policy advice · Think tanks

I had the good fortune to serve as President and CEO of the Stimson Center in its second decade, and at the start of the twenty-first century, from 2002 to 2015. Founded in 1989 by defense intellectuals Barry Blechman and Michael Krepon as the Cold War was winding down, Stimson was well established as a nonpartisan think tank on selected international security issues when I arrived in 2002. It was still a young organization, with a young staff, and open to some new ideas as the think tank community adapted to the new millenium.

Blechman and Krepon were prominent in national conversations about nuclear weapons policy, and Stimson also had made a name for itself on UN peace operations and UN reform, as well as respected regional security programs on China–Taiwan, and South Asia. Its early business model

E. Laipson (✉)
The Stimson Center, Washington, DC, USA

J. McGann, *The Future of Think Tanks and Policy Advice in the United States*, https://doi.org/10.1007/978-3-030-60386-1_5

was heavily focused on support from major US foundations, with less attention to corporate, government, or individual donors.

My role was to sustain the institution's well-established successes, and to expand our research portfolio and impact in the policy world. I had completed a quarter century of government service, largely in analytic and management positions at the Congressional Research Service and the National Intelligence Council. I had also served in policy positions at the State Department, the National Security Council staff, and at the US Mission to the UN. Throughout my career in government, I was in frequent contact with the robust community of think tanks in DC and beyond, whether as an observer or participant in task forces and events, or in more formal collaborations between government and nongovernment subject-matter experts.

Let me identify four themes that, in hindsight, reflect some of the changes to the think tank sector that affected Stimson and that, in some ways, Stimson tried to shape and influence: identifying new constituencies for our work driven by new technologies, expanding the research agenda to the evolving global agenda, navigating in an age of hyper-partisanship, and adapting to changing demographics in the workplace.

Technology-Driven Shifts in the Think Tank Marketplace

It seems a cliché to say that information technology and social media have transformed the communications' strategy for think tanks, but twenty years ago, not all think tanks were early adapters to the potential of online communication. For many think tanks, it was not self-evident that the internet would transform how think tanks reach their various audiences. It might be a curious addition to more traditional ways of disseminating studies, but many think tanks eventually realized they needed to pause and reflect on how to exploit the new technologies, and the consequences of the democratization of access to think tank production.

Most importantly for a small think tank like Stimson, the availability of these new tools did make us rethink whom we wanted to reach. Think tanks after all can rightly be viewed as elite organizations, where highly educated people with a passion for public policy work to provide fresh ideas or critical feedback to government officials. The greatest achievement of a think tank is to be recognized as the original source of a concept or plan that is embraced by leaders who can turn it into official policy, whether from Capitol Hill or an executive branch agency.

So it required some mental gymnastics to fully absorb the notion that think tank work could be made available to virtually anyone anywhere with the push of a button. When asked "who is your intended audience?" for a particular project or report, the answer suddenly became much harder to answer. Rather than naming a congressional committee or a unit of the national security bureaucracy, it had become possible at virtually no added cost to have multiple audiences, with consumers of our work whom we could not name or find on a map.

At an earlier think tank summit organized by the Think Tanks and Civil Society Program, a communications person at a major think tank explained the new strategy for disseminating a book: do a formal book launch with erudite conversation among public intellectuals, offer 500 word blog posts or 800 word opinion pieces to print and online media, and develop a plan to release a tweet every day for at least six months with a sentence from the book, at no more than 140 characters in length. The shorter the message, the larger the potential audience would be. Coming to grips with these diverse audiences forced us all to work harder to convey knowledge in clear prose to convey often complex ideas to expert as well as nonexpert readers.

Expanding Global Agenda for International Security

At the turn of the millennium, think tanks were also forced to refresh their research agendas. The post-Cold War era was already a decade old, and new, complex, transnational, and nontraditional problems were making their way onto the international security agenda. Former CIA director James Woolsey liked to refer to the transition from focusing on one big dragon to slay (the USSR) to coping with many snakes coiled around our ankles, not knowing which was lethal or most important. The terrorist attacks on September 1, 2001, instantly became the dominant threat, and the organizing principle for intelligence and law enforcement, and much of the defense and diplomatic efforts of the US government.

Think tanks followed suit, and many developed new programs to create databases and analytic work addressing terrorism and all of its policy ramifications. It took courage to buck this trend, and to assess the terrorism threat in context and perspective. Stimson did not create any new programming with terrorism as the primary focus, and instead established a new program on environmental security. Its first major endeavor was a listening tour of states around the Indian Ocean rim, to ascertain how climate change and other environmental issues affected their security policies and priorities. Developing countries with major cities along the ocean littoral nearly all placed climate change and sea level rise as their major security priority, more than territorial disputes or other conflicts with neighbors.

With Stimson's deep bench on nuclear issues, we had some lively discussions comparing the nuclear threat and that of climate change. Some believed that the use of nuclear weapons was the only true existential threat to the international system, but others would insist that the worst case scenarios related to climate change could well be more likely and have higher impact than the risks associated with nuclear weapons. In a graceful bridge across the two issue areas, Barry Blechman worked with the Wilson Center's Ruth Greenspan Bell to apply some lessons from nuclear arms control and disarmament during the Cold War to the emerging demand for global cooperation on climate change (Bell and Blechman 2012).

Partisanship's Effects on Policy Research

Stimson, like other independent think tanks, places its nonpartisan approach to international security issues at the core of its institutional identity. The board has former senior policy officials from administrations of both parties, and other business and civil society leaders who are not identified in a partisan manner at all. During my years at Stimson, sometimes that commitment to nonpartisanship accrued costs, whether in terms of limited access or influence on an incumbent administration, or in terms of funders who looked for champions of a particular worldview or approach to problem-solving. Sometimes it was lonely in the middle, as hyper-partisanship became a feature of our political culture.

But there were also ways to turn it into an advantage. We maintained a bipartisan program for congressional staff as long as we could find Democratic and Republican members willing to work together to sponsor information sessions on emerging national security issues. We were proud to provide a safe harbor for people looking for insights on major issues that were not presented through a political lens.

This is not to suggest that any think tank can control its reputation or avoid perceptions of political bias. Changes in the funding environment also contribute to think tanks being labeled as having a political agenda, or working to promote a benefactor's preferences, often with little or no basis for the accusation. Navigating the political landscape is only one of the challenges facing the think tank sector, and one that became more acute during my years at Stimson.

CHANGING DEMOGRAPHICS IN THE WORKPLACE

Another long-term change in the think tank world has been a long overdue expansion of staff to include women, minorities and other under-represented groups. Stimson was not the first think tank to have a woman president—Jessica Mathews became president of the Carnegie Endowment in 2001, as did Nancy Birdsall at the Center for Global Development. I joined Stimson a year later. We ranked exceptionally high in one assessment of women in leadership of the organization and of its research programs (Zenko 2011). A decade ago, Micah Zenko notes that Stimson was way ahead of other DC think tanks, with 50% of its leadership positions held by women.

During my tenure, many other women joined the ranks: Wendy Chamberlin at the Middle East Institute (2007–2018), Sarah Wartell at the Urban Institute (2012–present), Nancy Lindborg at USI (2015–2020), and Kay Cole James at Heritage in 2018.

Gender is not the only arena in which greater diversity is needed. African Americans and Hispanics are woefully underrepresented in think tank staff, and many other categories of workers could be better represented, so that think tanks do a better job reflecting the societies in which they work.

REFERENCES

SUBMISSIONS

Bell, Ruth Greenspan, and Berry Blechman. 22 December 2012. Global Warming Experts Should Think More About the Cold War. Wilson Center. https://www.wilsoncenter.org/article/global-warming-experts-should-think-more-about-the-cold-war.

Zenko, Micah. 14 July 2011. City of Men. *Foreign Policy*. https://foreignpolicy.com/2011/07/14/city-of-men/.

Current Presidents

Achieving Inclusivity by Redefining the Think Tank Scholar

Victoria Herrmann

Abstract Victoria Herrmann, President and Managing Director of The Arctic Institute in Washington, DC, explores the Future of Think Tanks and Policy Advice in the United States.

Keywords Policy advice · Think tanks

In 1675, Sir Isaac Newton wrote, "If I have seen further than others, it is by standing upon the shoulders of giants." As a young leader of a young(er) organization, it is perhaps predictable that I look to America's giants in think tank history for inspiration. As a world war loomed globally and the Great Depression devastated households in every corner of the nation, America's earliest think tanks advised US government officials on which policies would result in the greatest return for society. The research and analysis of the Carnegie Endowment for International Peace, where I held my first job out of college as a Junior Fellow, and The Brookings Institute next door, helped to define the European Recovery Program and the United Nations Charter. In leading a top 100 think tank in America

V. Herrmann (✉)
The Arctic Institute, Washington, DC, USA

© The Author(s) 2021   49
J. McGann, *The Future of Think Tanks and Policy Advice
in the United States*, https://doi.org/10.1007/978-3-030-60386-1_6

in 2019, I cast my gaze a century rearward to surmise how we too can inform the paramount policy decisions of today.

Of course, the enterprise of policy problem-solving has come a long way since the early days of advancing world peace and domestic policy progress. But the fundamental function of a think tank has not changed. Regardless of geography, discipline, or mission, a think tank continues to be a place, physical or virtual, where people come together to resolve the public's most pressing challenges. As an organization that creates spaces to activate ideas through the networking of individuals, it serves as the ultimate incubator for change. Think tanks ought to, at their core, expand what problems society thinks are possible to solve by paving new pathways for intellectuals to work together. In order to achieve this aspiration, think tanks must ensure that their organizational strategies foster inclusive management structures, research groups, and networks that reflect those whom they seek to serve.

Nonetheless, too often the composition of think tank teams and leadership in the twenty-first century still mirror those of their earliest ancestors in the 1910s and 1920s, when scholarship, governance, and civic engagement at large in the United States purposefully excluded people of color, women, people with low incomes, and people with disabilities. In the 2018 Global Go To Think Tank Index produced by the University of Pennsylvania's Lauder Institute, I was one of only 14 women leaders in the top 75 ranked US think tanks, and then at 28 years old, I was the youngest of all 75. These numbers look more austere for women of color. The biggest challenge, then, for think tanks today is to devise strategies that build, strengthen, and sustain diverse organizational structures. America's think tank leaders today must not only achieve the same quality and high-level policy influence of those early years; but they must also simultaneously invest in systemic change in their institutions so as to advance diversity, inclusion, and a multidisciplinary approach. In this, technology, politics, and the policy environment of today can buttress the dual goal of impact and empowerment.

Over the past century, innovations in technology and communications have democratized the sharing of ideas, and have given think tanks the tools to both reach new audiences and elevate new voices.

The Arctic Institute, the think tank for which I currently serve as Managing Director, has internalized inclusivity and diversity as organizational values and embraced low-cost web platforms, communication tools, and participatory research approaches to achieve our vision of creating a just, sustainable, and secure Arctic region.

USING ONLINE PUBLICATIONS TO ELEVATE NOT EXCLUDE

Online publishing on think tank websites must promote the work of their own research assistants, fellows, and leadership personnel—but they need not stop there. In over 80 commentaries, reports, infographics, and articles, The Arctic Institute brought together career diplomats, scientists, youth leaders, practitioners, and academics in a vibrant virtual dialogue on some of the most pressing challenges and promising opportunities of the circumpolar north. The Arctic Institute's *Breaking the Arctic's Ice Ceiling* series highlighted the work of women working and living in the Arctic. In recent years, women researchers, scientists, and local champions have elevated their visibility and empowered their voices across the world. The Arctic is no exception. With powerful organizations like *500 Women Scientists* and local movements like *Women in Polar Science* and *Plan A* growing their reach and impact, women are sharing their personal narratives, highlighting their contributions, and supporting each other like never before. The Arctic Institute's Breaking the Arctic's Ice Ceiling is our team's contribution to this movement. Allowing all types of scholars and storytellers to contribute to our series underscored the diversity of women leadership in the Arctic, instead of limiting submissions to those with higher education degrees and conventional career paths. From women climate change champions to being vegans at sea, we are using our publishing platform to elevate a more inclusive Arctic dialogue.

An *Indigenous Languages* series later in the year similarly amplified the expertise, personal narratives, and important contributions of both traditional knowledge holders and community-based scholars. Languages play a crucial role in both social and cultural development. They are intimately linked to people's own sense of identity, to their lands, and to their environments. In line with the United Nations' 2019 International Year of Indigenous Languages, The Arctic Institute's *Indigenous Languages in the Arctic* celebrated the linguistic and cultural diversity of Indigenous languages across the North. In a series of articles, commentaries, and op-eds, the contributing authors seek to raise awareness about the challenges and opportunities facing Indigenous languages and to highlight the immense value of linguistic diversity across the Circumpolar North. Uplifting the writing and experiences of Indigenous scholars in the predominately white space of policy think tanks is critical not only to purposefully change the knowledge landscape of publications today, but also showing a more diverse cohort of future scholars a pathway to engaging in think tank work.

SUPPORTING TEAM INCLUSIVITY BY VIRTUAL FLEXIBILITY

Without a centralized headquarter building that houses all scholars, the Arctic Institute brands itself as a think tank for the twenty-first century. In 2018, our network of multidisciplinary scholars worked and lived in 18 cities, 12 countries, and five continents, and represented expertise in many different disciplines. In order to accommodate a geographically, linguistically, and disciplinarily diverse team, we choose to invest in virtual infrastructure that not only brings us together but also provides points of lift for new ideas. The Arctic Institute uses Slack, a cloud-based instant messaging platform, for both direct communication within team working groups and our virtual monthly Arctic Water Cooler Discussions to engage external Arctic colleagues in lively policy discussions. To plan across continents, Trello allows us to create boards, lists, and cards to organize and prioritize projects. And for face-to-face meetings to these platforms, Zoom enhances our team's cohesion and interconnectedness.

Rather than spend on the overhead of a headquarters, a virtual think tank structure frees up funding for programming, personnel support, and targeted outreach to build audiences and influence policy. Holding live events, including roundtables, panels, and speaker engagements, is a challenge without a physical headquarters. However, this forces The Arctic Institute, and others who choose this path, to be more collaborative with other think tanks, nonprofit organizations, and universities, which in turn builds partnership bridges that might not have otherwise existed. And although it is difficult to build a community virtually rather than by socializing in an office setting, holding Zoom happy hours and professional development discussions helps to connect our team across continents. As the rapid transition to "Work from Home" schedules amidst the COVID-19 crisis in Spring 2020 illuminated, much of the in-person work conducted by think tanks can occur virtually, and some functions can be enhanced through a virtual option. For example, an additional co-benefit of virtual work is that the flexibility of telework supports a healthy work–life balance for many different types of lifestyles. This flexibility is critical to growing a diverse team where individuals can choose the place and schedule of work that best fits their responsibilities, from being an active parent to being a reindeer herder. The Arctic Institute is able to support its team regardless of where geographically or with which time-schedule they are basing their daily work. If the Institute were to require a critical mass of scholars to be headquartered in Washington, DC with a physical building, we would lose our scholars who live in the Arctic, enriching their research with lived experiences, and those who spend significant fieldwork time in the high north, like those who research wildlife–human settlement interactions in remote Arctic landscapes to produce policy recommendations directly from the field.

Ditching Desk Research
for a Participatory Action Approach

In order to inform the creation policy for a just, sustainable, and secure world in an era of rapid change, think tanks must strive toward evermore impactful and inclusive programming. It is no longer enough to conduct rigorous research that is transactional in nature between those studying and those being studied. Research must be tied to meaningful action. To meet current challenges of translating research into action, think tanks must consider a structural change to embrace the think-and-do-tank model.

One way to approach this structural transition is for think tanks to explore the Participatory Action Research model, a "research paradigm within the social sciences which emphasizes collaborative participation of trained researchers as well as local communities in producing knowledge directly relevant to the stakeholder community" (Coghlan and Brydon-Miller 2014). Participatory action can provide a pathway to move think tanks beyond tokenism of marginalized groups in research and representation. It does this by grounding collective inquiry in experience and social history, and implements research methods through a cyclic or spiral process which alternates between action and critical reflection.

A 2017–2018 Arctic Institute research project, *The Future of Rural Energy and Human Development*, used the Participatory Action Research approach to identify challenges and solutions surrounding the financial, political, and technical problems rural communities face when transitioning from primarily diesel fueled off-grid systems to renewable energy at the local level. On average, Arctic residents pay twice as much as their southern counterparts for heating, electricity, and transportation fuel. For those living in the Arctic, petroleum fuel isn't about global commodity markets: it's about survival. The need to support and foster the growth of small-scale, affordable clean energy projects in the Arctic is integral to alleviating poverty in these communities, to augmenting public health in the face of black carbon, and to safeguarding a carbon-neutral future to keep global warming below 2 degrees Celsius. At a two-day Symposium in Whitehorse, Yukon (Canada) in March 2017 held by The Arctic Institute, Arctic community champions, policymakers, and researchers from Alaska and Northern Canada convened to address this challenge and identify solutions to support future penetration of small-scale renewable energy. By rooting the interactive symposium in community experiences in the present and in a colonized past, and by holding the event in the Arctic rather than Ottawa or Washington, DC, the conversation and research products were directly relevant to both policymakers and local implementers.

REIMAGINING THE FUTURE THINK TANK SCHOLAR

At the core of these structural and strategy changes is a single challenge for think tanks today, and in the future: redefining what a think tank scholar looks like.

If think tanks are to stay relevant to policymakers and the public alike, their leadership must re-imagine the relationship between the type-cast experts of academic scholars and government officials, and those specialists yet to be fully engaged as experts in the field. It will require the presidents and executive management of organizations to look back and acknowledge past exclusions and discrimination; to look inward at their present structure to pinpoint current shortcomings in promoting equitable opportunity of employment and advancement for all types of experts; and to look forward and invest in a future strategy that makes meaningful, systemic change in representation, support, and maintenance of a better, wide-ranging team of scholars. This may include implementing the examples detailed above, or investing in new positions to include nontraditional knowledge holders and youth experts in the analysis of and engagement with public policy debates.

To act ambitiously on the greatest environmental, security, and economic policy issues of our time, think tanks must have the courage to simultaneously pursue the development of diverse teams that can put research into cooperative action. Being purposeful in including youth, women, scholars of color, and experts with nontraditional credentials. This is no easy task and will require the involvement of think tank presidents and human resource directors alike. But it is essential if think tanks are to be relevant in the ever-evolving policy and social landscape of the twenty-first century.

REFERENCE

Coghlan, David, and Mary Brydon-Miller. 2014. *The Sage Encyclopedia of Action Research*. London, UK: Sage.

Think Tanks Breaching the Partisan and Geopolitical Divide

Kevin Rudd

Abstract Kevin Rudd, President of the Asia Society Policy Institute in New York, NY, explores the Future of Think Tanks and Policy Advice in the United States.

Keywords Civil society · Disinformation campaigns · Fundraising · Policy advice · Policy analysis · Think tanks

We are living in turbulent times, rife with serious global challenges and opportunities—ranging from great power relations, to global pandemics, to climate change, and beyond. Think tanks, or as in the case of the Asia Society Policy Institute which I lead, "think- and do-tanks" have never been more important. We are also facing a time of both serious challenge and opportunity. On one hand, we must combat a lack of capacity, human resources, funding, and low audience attention spans, while also contending with fake news. On the other hand, there is increased demand for data-driven analysis and innovative solutions to new and enduring problems.

K. Rudd (✉)
Asia Society Policy Institute, New York, NY, USA

© The Author(s) 2021   57
J. McGann, *The Future of Think Tanks and Policy Advice
in the United States*, https://doi.org/10.1007/978-3-030-60386-1_7

We are in a new era of public policymaking, of polarization, and the playing of politics—which has changed for the worse ever since I was Prime Minister of Australia only about a decade ago (2007–2010; 2013). Given the shortening of the news cycle and greater social atomization, political leaders are now too often focused on both political and policy crisis management, instead of the core policy agenda of their governments. For policymakers, there is an imperative to survive the immediate, which means officials aren't always thinking about medium- to long-term policy challenges and solutions.

So where in this morass—which we call contemporary democratic politics—is the role of think tanks in the current and future policy debate?

Think tanks, comprising experts and practitioners, are well poised to develop policy ideas and solutions that political leaders from any party or government may lack. Indeed, at their core, regardless of the ethos of a think tank, these organizations should be in the business of dispassionate analysis, bearing out evidence-based policy recommendations and, where appropriate, political/policy roadmaps.

Of course, think tanks can still have an ethos, as well as hundreds of different ideas and policy solutions resulting from data and research that policymakers and stakeholders will feel best to address the problem. After all, the contestation of ideas is the best way to improve them.

The concern I have is that policy institutes may join others who are retreating to their corners in our increasingly polarized societies, focused on immediate political management, and ignoring the policy challenges of tomorrow. With this political expediency, there is tacit (or perhaps overt) approval to blur the line between analysis and editorial. With the increase in polarization, basic facts and science are being called into question, and objectivity is suffering. For example, one can credibly debate how best to mitigate climate change, but to deny that the global climate is changing in order to provide talking points to partisan policymakers to that effect undermines the public good that should be resulting from the work of think tanks; it undermines evidence and truth. Even using the same term—think tank—to categorize those who do dispassionate policy research and analysis and present evidence-based solutions, with those who serve as partisan communications consultants, erodes the independence and credibility of independent think tanks. This poses yet another challenge at a time when we are already rife with nonfact-based news, and are only beginning to contend with the rise of deep disinformation campaigns. As a society, we don't have the luxury of allowing a myriad of institutions to join in this dangerous game of politics.

Indeed, the sector has changed over the years, and for the most part, even with its challenges, it's changed mostly for the better. According to Jim McGann's research at the University of Pennsylvania, there are over 8000 think tanks around the world. Given this competition and the democratization of debate via technology, gone are the days of academicians alone providing analysis and solutions. The sector has (albeit slowly) made way for greater inclusion and diversity of backgrounds and experiences. But the medium has had to change along with the message, and subject-matter experts and practitioners now have to either be digital experts to push forth analysis and solutions into the wider public debate or think tanks need to have the resources to hire multimedia producers and marketers so that their ideas reverberate outside of a single echo chamber.

A significant human resource challenge also remains in the composition of senior think tank experts, at least in the United States, being mostly white, middle-aged males (and in full disclosure, I fit this categorization). The pipeline needs to change to bring in new voices and perspectives—which means that funding should be prioritized to offer paid internships, establish real mentorships, and provide professional development to bring new leaders up the ladder.

To change the way the bottom line is prioritized brings the challenge of think tank funding to the fore. As an independent think tank, we work to raise funds for project support so that we can engage in policy analysis and put forward inclusive recommendations. Project support covers the direct expenses associated with this work, and there is often a thin margin of support for staffing, as well as for keeping the lights turned on. Thus, fundraising also has to kick in for unrestricted support to run a not-for-profit think tank—while maintaining the independence and integrity of the work at the fore.

The opportunities for the think tanks of the future lie in addressing these challenges—furthering inclusion, pushing forward evidence-based solutions and resisting greater polarization, and in leveraging technology as a means toward these ends.

Staffing, affiliated experts, task forces, policy dialogues, public panels, and the like should be inclusive of differing viewpoints, cultures, areas in which expertise was obtained (academics, practitioners, and other stakeholders), genders, ages, political affiliations, etc. Inclusion and representation are key for problem-solving think tanks who are working to create effective solutions to today's challenges—regardless of issue area or region of focus.

The need to bring in and engage differing viewpoints is why technology has changed the way think tanks have had to work. The democratization of information brings with it a more informed and engaged public from all across the world, who will access information differently and utilize it in the public debate. Studies can't just be published as another tome to pass around capitals along with briefings to policymakers and stakeholders. A think tank's policy analysis and policy roadmaps must come with tailored shorter-form web content, data visualizations (ideally interactive), events, videos, podcasts, social media communications, engagement with traditional and new media, and so forth. And this may also need to be in multiple languages, and on multiple platforms, depending on what is utilized in the countries on which the work is focused.

There must also be an eye to what's next in technology and the consumption of information—so that independent, nonprofit think tanks don't end up decades behind other information-sharing platforms. The creation of content for these channels can be costly and thus, instead of each think tank trying to create it all, there is significant value in partnerships with other think tanks, media organizations, or other stakeholders to create joint products. By utilizing each other's work, pushing out information to broader networks, engaging different audiences interactively, and affecting change across a greater space, our evidence-based work can reach beyond the individual silos we've each created, and beyond partisan and polarized divides.

While I lead a think- and do-tank headquartered in the United States, I truly believe the future of think tanks across the world lies in reminding our citizens and fellow countrymen why challenges that seem far off or far away really aren't. Nor are the policy solutions needed to address them. Trade wars, climate disasters, recessions, ecocide, global pandemics, hot wars, cyberwars, refugee crises—in our interdependent world, these directly or indirectly affect us all.

Ultimately, for those think tanks who are independent and nonpartisan, we are a sector that serves civil society, policy, and journalism; we are repositories of research, hot-beds of analysis, and creators of and advocates for policy solutions. As we move forward, we must remind ourselves of this, and ask ourselves how do we remain useful for these audiences? How do we engage with them? How do we work together to effect change? How do we in substance, not in rhetoric, actually move the public policy dial?

The future of think tanks is about the future of dispassionate analysis, the future of inclusive and evidence-based problem-solving, and how much we are willing to not just think, but also to act.

Reimagining the Think Tank Post COVID-19

Frederick Kempe

Abstract Frederick Kempe, President and CEO of the Atlantic Council, Washington, DC, explores the Future of Think Tanks and Policy Advice in the United States.

Keywords Ivory tower · Policy advice · Think tanks · Transparency

Pandemics reveal fundamental truths about who we are as leaders, organizations, and a society. They expose our flaws and they accelerate trends.

Over the last decade at the Atlantic Council, the board and staff have been preparing for this moment through one of the most dramatic financial and programmatic turnarounds in American think tank history.

Though we didn't predict the test would be a global pandemic, we had prepared our staff and operations to navigate what we had identified as one of those periodic historic Inflection Points that would test our nation, our transatlantic community and our existing global order of rules and institutions.

F. Kempe (✉)
The Atlantic Council, Washington, DC, USA

J. McGann, *The Future of Think Tanks and Policy Advice in the United States*, https://doi.org/10.1007/978-3-030-60386-1_8

Every member of our worldwide think tank industry is navigating these unprecedented times without a roadmap. However, the Atlantic Council experience has lessons that are more broadly applicable.

It also provides insights into what we believe will be the inevitable reimagining of the think tank model for the post-COVID-19 world. It will require flatter organizations with more digital capability, more rapid decision-making and a future-oriented ethos that recognizes that a return-to-normal would be the riskiest path forward.

We have fared well thus far in these disruptive times, due to a well-articulated mission and strategy; a clear and accountable management structure; a diverse, nimble, entrepreneurial and results-oriented staff; a communications and program team with digital tools and tech know-how; and a committed community of generous donors, board directors and International Advisory Board members willing to contribute their wisdom and ensure financial stability.

Had COVID-19 struck a decade ago, we may have made our way through it, but we certainly would not be thriving and rising to the challenge as we have.

The steps the Atlantic Council took over the past decade in shaping its turnaround prepared us for this period that is testing our entire "industry." Within the story of how we got there lie lessons for any management team or board trying to decide whether to ramp up or wind down when facing existential challenges.

We came to COVID-19 with a fundamental belief: that the world confronted a defining moment as significant as were the periods following World Wars I and II. How we navigate this period will have historic consequences.

Our last strategic review was helpful to thinking this through. We landed on six defining challenges for our organization. Each now grows more important and urgent: navigating a new era of major competition; bolstering open market democracies; redefining and reinvigorating the United States' role in the world; strengthening the global system of rules and institutions; harnessing emerging technologies for good; and advancing global resilience through interrelated climate, migratory and—increasingly now—public health issues.

We believe that if the United States rises to this moment, alongside its partners and allies, we can navigate this period successfully and enter one of humanity's most enlightened and prosperous times. Conversely, we will pay a heavy price should we fail in our efforts.

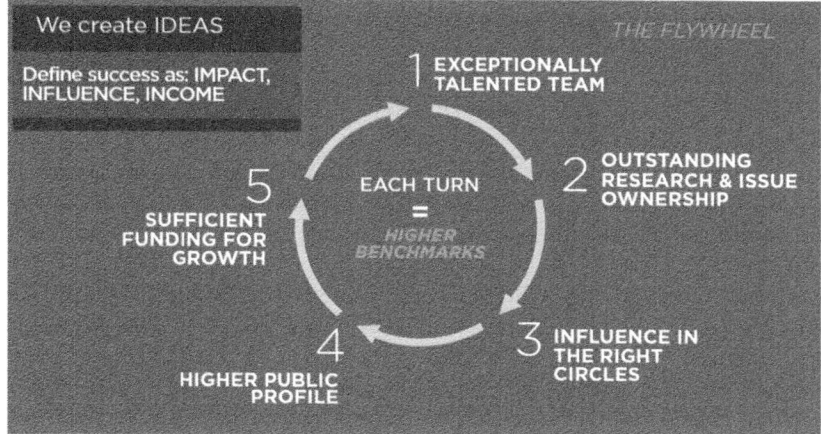

Fig. 1   Defining and measuring our success through impact, influence and income

As with other think tanks, COVID-19 has only brought everything we were doing into sharper relief.

While many around the world are "chasing the virus," we decided early on that our focus instead would be on the impact it had on our six defining challenges. That has kept our team focused—and our community clear on why we exist.

Our work at "shaping the global future" alongside allies and partners has never been more relevant and urgent. Our secret sauce coming into this historically challenging time was having the right agenda and culture to execute this mission.

Among the many impacts of this unprecedented public health and economic crisis has been its ability to highlight the strengths and weaknesses of all institutions. As I told our team in our first Zoom town hall at the end of our initial week of telework in March 2020—with 170 individuals across a dozen time zones on the line—we will either increase our relevance during coronavirus or we will risk irrelevance thereafter.

Measures we took to "turn around" the Atlantic Council over the past decade weren't designed with a global pandemic in mind. Yet what began for us with an "impact flywheel" in 2007—a simple device that could work for any nonprofit (Fig. 1)—ended with an organization that had all the elements in place to operate virtually, perhaps even more effectively than we performed as an office-bound team.

At the center of our flywheel were the "four Is" that had to drive all our thinking: (actionable) Ideas, (policy) Influence, (public) Impact, and (sustainable) Income.

Our flywheel had at its apex "TALENT," as nothing is more important in a business that produces primarily intellectual capital. It all begins with hiring gifted "culture carriers" to advance the work and ensure the culture.

Move to the right and the next requirement is "DIFFERENTIATED FOCUS," which requires consistently posing the question, "what can our institution do better than all others?"

Move further around the flywheel clockwise and you land upon "INFLUENCE ON DECISION MAKERS," the more traditional work of think tanks. If you want to shape outcomes, you must not only reach top policymakers but also give them reason to listen.

Yet even that is insufficient.

As one travels further to the other side of the flywheel, we discovered a new element for Atlantic Council work that was crucial for our times: "IMPACT ON THE PUBLIC DEBATE." It is seldom enough any longer to throw out weighty papers or launch lofty projects from an ivory tower and expect results, unless one is prepared to advocate for them publicly.

The last stop on the flywheel, before returning to the top, is quite simply and crucially "INCOME."

None of the rest can be done without it. As General James L. Jones, the two-time chairman of the Atlantic Council likes to say, "Vision without resources is hallucination."

We initially saw our lack of a sizable endowment, a situation shared by many think tanks in our community, as a potentially fatal flaw.

Instead, however, it has made us more dynamic, innovative, responsive, and entrepreneurial. We have found that our strict adherence to intellectual independence, transparency regarding donors and well-established and enforced ethical standards has been attractive to our donors (or "investors" in our mission, as I like to call them).

The attached timeline (Fig. 2) of Atlantic Council innovations over the past dozen years, with a fever chart of revenue growth, underscores the value of sustainable innovation for any think tank. Named centers and fellows, in particular, unlocked the value of the Atlantic Council: Adrienne

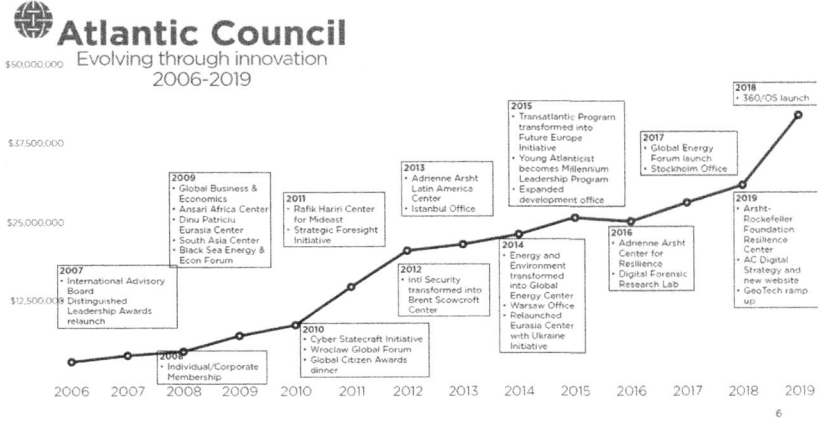

Atlantic Council
Evolving through innovation
2006-2019

Fig. 2 Over the last 12 years, the Atlantic Council has experienced tremendous programmatic expansion with consistent year-over-year revenue growth

Arsht, Brent Scowcroft, Bahaa Hariri, and Boyden Gray being the most prominent of the current group.

What we also learned is that the board chair position was fundamental to ensuring consistency of purpose and leadership. The Atlantic Council has enjoyed four significant chapters of board leadership in the last dozen years, serving to reorient the institution and remake it as a global leader.

Since 2006, the position has been held by Ambassador Henry Catto, General (ret.) James L. Jones (twice), Senator (later Defense Secretary) Chuck Hagel, General (ret.) Brent Scowcroft (long the organization's driving force), General Jones again and, now, for our crucial new era, John Rogers.

The current executive vice chairs of the board, Adrienne Arsht and Steve Hadley, have inspired the work of other board members. Ms. Arsht has done this through funding and founding two Atlantic Council Centers. Mr. Hadley leads the frequent and intensive revisiting and refreshing of our strategy to readjust to the changing landscape.

Yet we have never lost sight of the reality that the "why" of the Atlantic Council could never work without the "who" and the "what"—the talent of the organization and what they uniquely could offer to a demanding world.

With each turn of the flywheel, we try to lift the bar for ourselves: hiring more capable talent, sharpening our programmatic focus, deepening our influence on decision-makers through the quality of our work, shaping the public debate through the improvements in our communications, and creating more sustainable financing through a stronger development team seeking larger, more strategic multiyear gifts.

During my twenty-five years as a Wall Street Journal editor and reporter before joining the Atlantic Council, few stories captured my attention more than business turnarounds. The best of them were rich yarns that captured how entrepreneurial chief executives and their risk-taking boards stepped into reverse corporate fortunes in the face of daunting obstacles and demanding markets.

There are far fewer such stories in the nonprofit think tank world, given the absence of risk capital and private sector financial incentives, as well as the established belief among many that activity and output like an event or report are of sufficient impact themselves.

In that spirit, the story of the Atlantic Council turnaround is worth telling in some detail for what others might learn from it when their organization is stuck in a nonproductive rut or is struggling with financial headwinds.

As of end-2019, the growth from the beginning of 2007 to 2019 has been 13-fold in revenues, 17-fold in assets and an expansion to 14 from 5 programs and centers. As a result, the Atlantic Council has enjoyed an immeasurable increase in its ability to perform its mission.

What we've learned is that think tank turnarounds can only be achieved if the fundamental mission ("the product") is sufficiently compelling and unique, and thus "marketable;" if the board is willing to take risks and assist with business development; and if the handful of top managers are themselves entrepreneurial.

The most crucial board debate we faced during the turnaround was whether we should focus our mission entirely on transatlantic affairs, with a specific focus on NATO, or whether we should, as we ultimately decided to do, broaden our remit globally, with the argument that the transatlantic community could not succeed if it didn't itself tackle global challenges together.

What we were slow to learn, but now try to implement more consistently, is that it is just as important that the entire staff be recruited in accordance with a dominant set of cultural characteristics. For us they were intellectual entrepreneurship, collegiality (as we must work as a team), optimism (as we must believe we can shape the world), expertise (you need to know your field to influence it) and results-orientation (you must know how to get things done).

We like to quote the anthropologist Margaret Mead when our critics say we expect too much of our still relatively small organization.

"Never doubt that a small group of thoughtful, committed citizens can change the world," she said. "Indeed, it's the only thing that ever has."

No think tank has achieved great things by aiming too low.

The Challenges of Regulating Technology and the Role of Think Tanks in Informing Sound Tech Policy

Edward P. Djerejian and Moshe Y. Vardi

Abstract Edward P. Djerejian, Director and Moshe Y. Vardi, Faculty Scholar at the Baker Institute for Public Policy Houston, TX, explore the Future of Think Tanks and Policy Advice in the United States.

Keywords Policy advice · Public health crisis · Think tanks · University-affiliated

The principal role of think tanks is to address the pressing public policy issues of the moment. Now that the world is grappling with the major public health crisis posed by COVID-19, think tanks are uniquely positioned to inform policy surrounding technology that can combat and alleviate this pandemic, all by prioritizing data-driven research and policy solutions over politicization and profit.

One of the most basic and urgent policy questions is how to tackle the rising role of technology—especially social media—in our public sphere. As social media has proliferated across the globe, societies have had to grapple with its implications for both exercising and constraining speech.

E. P. Djerejian (✉) · M. Y. Vardi
Baker Institute for Public Policy, Houston, TX, USA

J. McGann, *The Future of Think Tanks and Policy Advice in the United States*, https://doi.org/10.1007/978-3-030-60386-1_9

71

While social media has provided a platform for countless individuals to express their opinions, many argue that social media companies must become more accountable for harmful content published on their sites. In the context of these concerns, there is a tech-policy vacuum to fill, and think tanks are positioned to fill it with dispassionate, fact-driven analysis of a complex, politically contentious subject.

While it is imperative that policymakers provide oversight to the tech sector on behalf of the public, the fast-growing scope of social media technology poses a huge policy challenge. Think tanks cannot resolve, for instance, fundamental philosophical differences on the proper way to meet the challenge. They can, however, help lawmakers to understand technical complexities, evaluate policy proposals, and provide for open debate and exchange of ideas regarding technology.

The case of Facebook provides a timely illustration of the salience of technological change in the world of social media. Facebook CEO Mark Zuckerberg's recent call for increased regulation of the Internet sidestepped perhaps the most significant question at hand: Is Facebook's business model the real problem? And, if so, is it redeemable?

Over the last several years, Facebook has been involved in a series of controversial issues. Consider this small sample:

- Cambridge Analytica harvested the personal data of millions of people's Facebook profiles without their consent and used it for political purposes.
- Facebook gave big companies access to its users' data without users' permission.
- UK lawmakers published internal Facebook emails that paint a picture of a company continuously seeking ways to monetize vast amounts of personal data collected from users.
- A Facebook software bug may have affected close to seven million people who used a Facebook login and gave permission to third-party apps to access their photos.

In response to the bad publicity accompanying these disclosures, Zuckerberg wrote a *Washington Post* op-ed calling for increasing regulation of the Internet in four areas: harmful content, election protection, effective privacy and data protection, and data portability.

Until 2014, Facebook's motto was: "Move fast and break things. Unless you are breaking stuff, you are not moving fast enough" (Murphy 2014). Despite the benefits of innovation and change, "breaking things" can have profound and dangerous unintended consequences. The argument that social media has become an instrument for undermining democracy is a strong one. It is also now widely accepted that during 2016 social media seriously affected the 2016 Brexit referendum in Britain and the presidential election in the United States. It is this cavalier attitude about breaking things that led *Wall Street Journal* columnist Peggy Noonan to describe Silicon Valley executives as "moral Martians" (Noonan 2017). New Zealand's privacy commissioner went so far as to describe Facebook as "morally bankrupt" for failing to efficiently remove live-streamed footage of the Christchurch massacre (Doffman 2019).

Ethan Zuckerman, director of the MIT Center for Civic Media, has called the advertising-based business model the "original sin" of the Internet, as "free" services to consumers are really funded by consumers, albeit in a relatively opaque way (Zuckerman 2014). But market opaqueness is only one problem. As we now know, internet advertisers require data to ensure effective delivery of ads. Thus, users not only pay for "free information" with an invisible tax, but they also pay by providing their personal information. Thanks to the success of "surveillance capitalism," many fear that the internet has become a means to surveil individuals who are unaware of how their private data is being utilized.

A discussion of modern internet regulation requires mention of Section 230 of the Communications Decency Act of 1996, a fundamental piece of US legislation that provides immunity from liability for providers and users of an "interactive computer service" who publish information provided by third-party users. The law states: "No provider or user of an interactive computer service shall be treated as the publisher or speaker of any information provided by another information content provider" (Legal Information Institute). By allowing Facebook and other Internet companies to operate as a platform, rather than as a publisher, Section 230 frees them from liability for the content that they publish. The explosive growth of social media platforms would have not been possible without Section 230. At the same time, it is doubtful that Congress could have conceptualized anything similar to today's social media in 1996. One can argue that Facebook is quite far from being a neutral platform because of its algorithm-based system that generates content based on users' preferences.

Social media's rapid growth has led to widespread manipulation. By co-opting social media platforms, unscrupulous actors ranging from disgruntled individuals to state-run intelligence operations have found a ready way to distribute false, misleading, and hateful content to millions of people. But it is no longer possible to believe that the proliferation of bad content on the Internet is a mere exercise of "free speech"; indeed, the murder of Heather Heyer in Charlottesville, Virginia, the synagogue massacre in Pittsburgh, and the mosque massacre in Christchurch, New Zealand can all be tied in some way to incendiary rhetoric propagated on online platforms.

In fact, this proliferation of "bad speech" on social media platforms has become politically untenable, and now all social media platforms are actively fighting "bad speech." Recently, for example, social media platforms banned conspiracy theorist Alex Jones for violating their "abusive behavior" policy. Thus, in spite of Section 230, social media platforms seem to be accepting responsibility for the content they publish. In other words, they are starting to behave with some restraint, like publishers, rather than platforms.

It is not at all clear, however, whether a platform like Facebook, which also owns Instagram and WhatsApp, with more than 2.5 billion active users, can behave like a traditional publisher. First, there is the difficulty of vetting content from a large quantity of users. With fewer than 40,000 employees, Facebook clearly cannot have humans review all its content; algorithmic filtering is a must. But, if we have learned anything over the last few years, it is how good people are at outsmarting algorithms. Facebook removed 1.5 million videos of the Christchurch attacks within 24 hours, yet many archived versions remain available (Mahtani 2019).

More fundamentally, do we really want Facebook to regulate the speech of more than 2.5 billion people? No government in the world has such power to regulate the speech of almost a third of humanity. Of course, traditional publishers regulate speech on their platforms, but there is a multiplicity of such outlets with no single authority having a monopoly on deciding for or against certain content. In contrast, there is only *one* Facebook.

The fundamental policy question of how to regulate speech on social media platforms seems inseparable from another policy concern, namely how to deal with the concentration of power in technology. The five largest US corporations are all tech companies—Alphabet, Amazon, Apple, Facebook, and Microsoft—and have a combined market capitalization of over four trillion dollars. For this reason, the tech sector is often called "Big Tech" these days. Furthermore, a small number of corporations have come to dominate the IT industry, as within each industry segment one corporation often eclipses the others. There are several initiatives underway to regulate tech. The biggest regulatory issue on the table is how to deal with overly dominant corporations. In the 2018 book, *The Curse of Bigness: Antitrust in the New Gilded Age*, legal scholar Tim Wu argues that the United States must enforce antitrust laws against such corporations (Szalai 2018).

Beyond the matter of regulating online content and the practices of tech corporations, it is imperative that policymakers be holistically informed about the broad landscape of technological innovation. Indeed, from 1972 to 1995, the Office of Technology Assessment (OTA) existed to supply members of Congress with analysis on a range of technology-related questions. Recently, a bipartisan group of legislators has pushed to reinvigorate the OTA in 2020, with one such proponent, Rep. Mark Takano (D-CA), remarking that "for more than two decades the OTA […] provid[ed] relevant, unbiased technical and scientific assessments for Members of Congress and staff" (IPWatchdog 2019). Nevertheless, in the absence of such a governmental office and in the event that it is not refunded, it is incumbent upon think tanks to provide policymakers with nonpartisan analysis on the tech landscape, both nationally and globally.

Technology is one of the most potent forces driving societal change today, but without reasonable national and international regulatory policies within this sector, it is not clear who is doing the steering. The coronavirus pandemic that has shocked the globe in 2020 has further borne witness to the fact that innovative advancements in the private sector do not always align with public needs in a time of crisis, especially when corporations are tempted to produce vital technology in jurisdictions with less burdensome regulations. This is perhaps best exemplified by calls to end China's supply-chain domination for life-saving medical technology and equipment and to relocate the production of such technology to the United States, where it can be more conveniently regulated and distributed (Beavers 2020). Policymakers have finally recognized that while they should allow the free market to innovate, technology must ultimately be appropriately overseen by governments, subject to democratic political processes. Even so, they are hampered by the dearth of well-studied policy alternatives. While the risks of leaving technology unregulated are becoming clearer by the day, there are also risks of rushing forward with regulation, the consequences of which are difficult to foresee.

In sum, the role of think tanks in addressing this issue and providing objective analysis and policy recommendations to decision-makers should be a high priority. In many ways, university-affiliated think tanks, such as Rice University's Baker Institute for Public Policy, have a comparative advantage in addressing these issues, as they have scientific expertise at immediate hand among the faculty of the universities where they are based.

References

Submissions

Beavers, Olivia. 5 April 2020. Momentum Grows to Change Medical Supply Chain from China. *The Hill.* https://thehill.com/policy/national-security/491119-momentum-grows-to-change-medical-supply-chain-from-china.

Doffman, Zak. 8 April 2019. Facebook Slammed as 'Morally Bankrupt, Pathological Liars' as Regulation Becomes Real. *Forbes.* https://www.forbes.com/sites/zakdoffman/2019/04/08/facebook-slammed-as-morally-bankrupt-pathological-liars-for-not-acting-on-live-streaming/#17ec0c64200f.

IPWatchdog. 20 September 2019. Bipartisan Effort to Resurrect Office of Technology Assessment Introduced. https://www.ipwatchdog.com/2019/09/20/bipartisan-effort-resurrect-office-technology-assessment-introduced/id=113584.

Mahtani, Shibani. 17 March 2019. Facebook Removed 1.5 Million Videos of the Christchurch Attacks Within 24 Hours—And There Were Still Many More. *The Washington Post.* https://www.washingtonpost.com/world/facebook-removed-15-million-videos-of-the-christchurch-attacks-within-24-hours–and-there-were-still-many-more/2019/03/17/fe3124b2-4898-11e9-b871-978e5c757325_story.html.

Murphy, Samantha. 30 April 2014. Facebook Changes Its 'Move Fast and Break Things' Motto. Mashable. https://mashable.com/2014/04/30/facebooks-new-mantra-move-fast-with-stability/.

Noonan, Peggy. 5 October 2017. The Culture of Death—And of Disdain. *The Wall Street Journal.* https://www.wsj.com/articles/the-culture-of-deathand-of-disdain-1507244198.

Szalai, Jennifer. 12 December 2018. A Look at Competition in Business Urges Us to Think Small. *The New York Times.* https://www.nytimes.com/2018/12/12/books/review-curse-of-bigness-antitrust-law-tim-wu.html.

Zuckerman, Ethan. 14 August 2014. The Internet's Original Sin. *The Atlantic.* https://www.theatlantic.com/technology/archive/2014/08/advertising-is-the-internets-original-sin/376041/.

Think Tanks and the Enduring Value of Hard Questions

Ash Carter

Abstract Ash Carter, Director of the Belfer Center for Science and International Affairs, Cambridge, MA, explores the Future of Think Tanks and Policy Advice in the United States.

Keywords Policy advice · Research centers · Think tanks

Think tanks face an uncertain future. An increasingly disintermediated information environment and rapid changes in revenue sources are just two of the many challenges that have compelled think tanks in the United States to reexamine their structure and strategy.

Amid this transition, it's worth reflecting on the enduring contributions that think tanks make to a democratic marketplace of ideas. They serve as:

- Bridges between academia and policymaking
- Independent sources of expertise and authority
- Safe spaces to define and debate policy ideas

A. Carter (✉)
Belfer Center for Science and International Affairs,
Cambridge, MA, USA

© The Author(s) 2021
J. McGann, *The Future of Think Tanks and Policy Advice
in the United States,* https://doi.org/10.1007/978-3-030-60386-1_10

- Conveners of stakeholders with diverse perspectives
- Originators of solutions to policy problems
- Mentors to future generations of public servants.

While political polarization and fragmentation of media may change the *way* think tanks carry out their mission, it does not fundamentally change the *need* for it. If anything, the value of research that's responsive to, but also independent from, public policy decision-makers has increased in this environment. This may sound counterintuitive at a time when observers see the rise of a post-truth, anti-elitist information space, but the ongoing demand for rigorous analysis of emerging challenges by congressional staffers, diplomats, state and local officials, scholars, journalists, business executives, students, and citizens suggests otherwise.

How should think tanks adapt and thrive in this changing landscape? They must chart a future with three coordinates: people, purpose, and products.

It's often said in Washington that "personnel is policy." So too is it with think tanks. The agendas we pursue, the issues we address, the relationships we form, the stakeholders we serve, the events we organize: all of these reflect, to a large degree, the scholars and staff we recruit and retain. Think tanks that pay lip service to diversity while continuing to feature panels of older white males won't just contend with bad optics—they will suffer a competitive disadvantage.

Think tanks must compete for talent. Those that develop the clearest career pathways for traditionally underrepresented populations will be best positioned to attract the next generation of think tank stars. Likewise, the old compartmentalization of scholars and administrators is no longer tenable or wise. Researchers must be capable of managing their own budgets, raising funds, running communications, and organizing events. And staff of all ages should be increasingly empowered to substantively contribute to programming. Such cross-training allows think tanks to do more with less.

There are several thousand think tanks in the United States, along with a growing number of law firms, advocacy groups, PR firms, consultancies, and for-profit think tanks that generate their own policy content. This proliferation is a net positive for the formation of ideas. At the same time, we should be clear-eyed about the risks of having so many producers of content primarily serving private or corporate interests, rather than the broad public interest. Think tanks exist to think, not advocate. When influence campaigns usurp research efforts as priorities, the quality, independence, and integrity of scholarship suffers.

Increased competition also requires traditional research centers to think more clearly about their value. Merely having a mission statement isn't sufficient. Instead, think tanks must also articulate a value proposition. What can they do first, best, uniquely, or only? Whether they're selling granola bars or software, for-profit firms must grapple with this. So, too, should think tanks.

In the case of Harvard Kennedy School's Belfer Center, it is the unique lens of science and technology that we bring to the study of international affairs. At the Belfer Center, we believe that the most potent levers of change to the security and prosperity of our world are science and technology. That conviction informs all of our work, and it serves as a competitive distinction.

Serious research projects can take months, even years. By now, most think tanks realize that sharing the findings of these projects in a formal report is necessary but woefully insufficient. The insights that populate such a report can also shape a blog post; a tweet; an op-ed; a policy brief; a podcast; a video; an infographic; a public event; and so on. And while think tanks are increasingly effective at disseminating these outputs broadly, there's still no substitute for traditional news media to carry the message to the public.

Engineers like to say that there are no bad materials, just bad applications. Which products think tanks use will depend on the audiences they seek to inform. But regardless of their form, they must all be accessible, credible, and memorable. Many think tank products fail this test because they neglect to connect research findings to real people. At the core of every policy reform is the assumption that it can help improve people's lives. Yet, too many publications never make that moral case, or bother to connect scholarship to the lives of citizens in practical ways. The leading think tanks of the future will combine the analytical rigor of first-rate scholarship with the storytelling craftsmanship of first-rate journalism.

Print newspapers that depended heavily on revenue from classifieds and car dealership ads faced a rude reckoning in the 2000s. Back then, publishers that saw the rise of Craigslist didn't realize that it could mean a serious, let alone existential, threat to their business model. Their failure of imagination led to one of the biggest industry shake-ups. Think tanks today may not face the same peril as did journalists (or travel agents) earlier this century, but the lesson holds: disruption emerges in surprising ways.

One dilemma many think tanks must resolve in the future relates to political volatility. Think tanks with clear partisan or ideological agendas may enjoy easier inroads to networks of like-minded donors. Indeed, the same incentives that have tended to enable extreme candidates to perform well in primary campaigns are also pushing think tanks to become more tendentious, and more focused on advocacy. At the same time, these organizations often struggle for influence when the opposing party controls the levers of government.

Think tanks that can credibly claim to serve the interests of citizens and government—not just parties and administrations—have the highest prospects for long-term impact. One way to ensure this credibility is to give individual scholars, not executives, the freedom and autonomy to pursue research agendas. Another is to avoid the temptation to constantly transform scholarship into a set of policy recommendations. Often, the greatest contribution an expert can make to a policy challenge is to more clearly define the problem. We live in an age that craves easy answers. But think tanks are uniquely positioned to ask hard questions. They should continue to do so.

The Future of Think Tanks: The Impact of Technology on Society

John Allen

Abstract John Allen, President of The Brookings Institution, Washington, DC, explores the Future of Think Tanks and Policy Advice in the United States.

Keywords Fundraising · Policy advice · Policy analysis · Think tanks

From the creation of the printing press to the harnessing of electricity, technological innovation has long been a driver for societal transformation. Yet today, with the advent of big data analytics, artificial intelligence, supercomputing, and other new and emerging technologies, the twenty-first century is increasingly being defined by radical, fast-paced change unlike anything before in modern history. In aggregate, these advances are leading us irrevocably toward a revolution in human affairs, where from the strategic to the grassroots of society, everything is changing. For the first time in decades, if not centuries, nearly every dimension of the human condition is being called into question, from sovereignty, governance and the rule-based world order, to the very nature of learning and the future of work. For the think tank community, this evolution

J. Allen (✉)
The Brookings Institution, Washington, DC, USA

© The Author(s) 2021   81
J. McGann, *The Future of Think Tanks and Policy Advice
in the United States*, https://doi.org/10.1007/978-3-030-60386-1_11

amounts to a seismic shift, raising serious foundational questions about everything—from the very nature of research to research priorities themselves, to communications strategies and digital infrastructure, and to development of interests and fundraising. In fact, many of these impacts are already being felt and will only grow in the years to come. If the think tank community is to retain its current role as a leading voice for public policy research and recommendations, adaptation to the technological realities of the twenty-first century—both in terms of what think tanks study as well as how they study it—is a strategic priority with existential implications.

Looking back on how we arrived at this current moment, much of today's technological trajectory began with the invention of the Internet and the formulation of data as its primary resource. This core technology—originally hailed as the "Information Superhighway" and a new means of generating shared understanding around the globe—quickly outpaced even the most liberal of estimates in terms of growth. Additionally, it began to influence societies around the world in major, yet, unforeseen ways. Moving forward to both the advent of social media—with billions of individuals now connected on an explosion of ever-evolving, network-capable platforms—and the introduction of the Internet of Things (IOT), connected masses of people on a 24/7 basis, and the true impacts of computing, big data, and the internet began to solidify and take shape. This profound linking of people, places, and environment—which also pushed data and its collection into nearly every aspect of daily life—amounted to what has today been described as the "digital revolution." And, almost immediately, governance became more complex, popular aspirations increased and became more demanding, and traditional concepts of national sovereignty began to change around the globe as more and more people became connected.

At its best, the digital revolution connected people and communities in beneficial ways that aligned with the original ideals and intent of the Internet. Perspectives, interests, and the sense of an interconnected global community grew, and business functions—such as international trade and shipping—began to streamline in an exponential manner. However, the emergence of major protest movements, such as the 2011 "Arab Spring," made it clear that this technological revolution had the ability to generate an altogether more complex form of impact: mass mobilization. With this revelation, movements began spreading around the world, with authoritarian regimes taking particular notice of the platforms and technologies that predicted these powerful societal movements. Surveillance networks and "fake news"—manufactured to sow confusion and dissent—soon followed, with authoritarian and illiberal regimes continuing to iterate on new tools and deployment strategies. These were aimed at both: controlling their own populations while maximizing their capacity to project their own malign influence and impact abroad.

The United States, the most technologically advanced country on the planet, was not even immune. These technologies underwrote Russia's strategic influence campaign against the United States and acted as a catalyst for political division, with the 2016 US presidential election being a prime example. In the time since, polarization and political fragmentation have dominated the media landscape and the overall tone of the nation. In addition, political extremes have slowly become normalized, and many ideas once thought to be radical—or even dangerous—have become mainstream through efforts to create false equivalencies between concepts with wildly different origins, standards of acceptance, and moral integrity. This era has sometimes been called the "post truth" environment or one of "truth decay," and in the present, no ideal or idea—even the core principles of democracy itself, is safe from predation and discontent.

Furthermore, at a truly strategic level, technology has led to the emergence of a new form of governance—that of digital sovereignty, which is a fundamentally reshaping concept for the formulation and implementation of public policy. With the tech sector generating many of the forces impacting the global community, its relevance and influence—and indeed its accumulation of vast wealth—has grown to such a significant extent that many entities now have the ability to impact entire societies. This is in both, a targeted sense and a manner that ignores borders, thus upending traditional concepts of sovereignty. What's more, these corporations— some of whom have "GDPs" far larger than that of some nations—now control the primary resource of the digital revolution—data—and thus the primary asset for the development of many of the most powerful emerging technologies, including artificial intelligence. In this new environment, tech corporations, armed with capabilities of their own making, are now beginning to reshape reality and the manner in which society governs itself. This is a profound evolution and challenges many of the core assertions of modern government and the social contract. All this also extends to the realities of the formulation of public policy. The policy environment is changing, the players are now very different, and the means to conduct policy research and analysis is evolving. Any one of these factors has been in play before, but never all three at the same time.

Despite the complex and disruptive nature of this new environment, there are clear opportunities for the think tank community to adapt and excel. Three points follow. First, with a tech sector that is generating a significant degree of societal change, improved engagement with leaders and organizations within this community would be highly beneficial toward driving future impact. At the 2020 World Economic Forum, for instance, it was tech sector leadership, not government officials, who drove many of the discussions, and certainly the overall tone of the convening. Unsurprisingly then, many were clamoring to engage with these same individuals—think tank leadership included. This community will become increasingly important in the years to come, and they'll need clear public policy research and analysis to inform their actions as they begin to tread into traditional policymaking spaces and engage directly with governments. In addition, these potential connections, networks, and partnerships would well-serve policymakers seeking to communicate directly with the tech sector on issues of shared importance. Here, the think tank community may in fact be able to serve as the "bridge" between these two communities and thus serve a greater array of entities and communities impacting the policy space. In fact, you are already seeing think tanks create initiatives specifically tied to the technology issues being driven by the Silicon Valley community, with Stanford's Institute for Human-Centered Artificial Intelligence often cited as one of the best and most successful models worthy of emulation.

A second opportunity for think tanks relates to that of "tech-fluency," or a general understanding of how technology issues are holistically impacting all policy spaces. Indeed, the nature of many emerging technologies is that no policy space is truly divorced from their impacts—thus, even a basic understanding of the nature of the technologies involved would greatly enhance research and analysis in all fields. What's more, the need for deep and "dual" policy expertise in both relevant public policy fields as well as in technologies like big data analytics and artificial intelligence will only grow as the years progress. Individuals with these skill sets are currently rare, yet their thinking and perspectives would add real value to so many critical policy fields. Here, think tanks have room to grow toward developing themselves into platforms that impact a wider array of communities—especially those that influence, or even decide, public policy outcomes. And, of course, improvements in tech-fluency would only improve the think tank community's ability to engage directly with the tech sector. Many younger scholars and staff grew up in an environment that gave them an implicit understanding of the important role technology plays in our daily lives, and the ways it can be incorporated into traditional policy spaces. At Brookings, we are already seeing the immense value of these individuals in adapting the way we do business—they are the future of our community and will be central to our ability to truly become "tech fluent."

Finally, a key opportunity area for think tanks is that of digital infrastructure. Big data analytics are slowly but surely defining significant portions of the analysis space, with their findings revealing important causalities that other methods might not detect. By upgrading these capabilities, think tanks would be able to accommodate new work streams and forms of analysis, as well as augment existing research products in novel ways. Investments in this area will also be essential in the long run, especially as the utilization of big data becomes more commonplace across all fields. Furthermore, digital infrastructure improvements would support a more comprehensive talent pipeline because individuals with the knowledge to use a skill set can make that organization a more attractive place to work. In so many fields of study, research communities, governments, and corporations alike have only just begun to capture information that could inform future policy decisions. That however will soon change—but only through the right infrastructure improvements will think tanks be able to harness this information for the good of their research, and through those efforts, the good of the global community.

For the think tank community, these three realities should constitute a cautionary tale. Previously, in this paper, the analogy was used of the think tank being a bridging solution between the reality of the changing nature of public policy, the needs of policymakers and deciders, and the nature of the tech sector and community. Because so few think tanks have evolved and adapted to take on such a bridge-building role, we're beginning to see universities and the tech sector itself creating their own capacities for conducting tech-related public policy research. The resourcing and funding dedicated for those capacities has been extraordinary—a trend that has not yet replicated itself to the same extent within the traditional think tank community, especially for digital infrastructure and other operational issues. Late moving think tanks in this area will struggle to compete in an increasingly dense field of research and analysis. As the think tank community moves deeper into the tech-dominated twenty-first-century public policy research landscape, the challenges of adapting and evolving to the broader policy ecosystem will be formidable—and for some, even existential.

Amidst this period of technological disruption, the value of public policy research takes on a new appearance and the think tank community remains an important source for independent and in-depth policy analysis and recommendations. As they have done in the past, the government and the general public alike are relying on think tanks to inform their thinking, especially in an age of increased disinformation, an active assault on truth, and democratic decay. Through investments in digital infrastructure, tech expertise, and tech sector engagement, this need will continue to be met, or even improved upon, in the foreseeable future and beyond.

Crowded, Chaotic, Contested: The New Geopolitical Order and Marketplace of Ideas

William Burns

Abstract William Burns, President of the Carnegie Endowment for International Peace, Washington, DC, explores the Future of Think Tanks and Policy Advice in the United States.

Keywords Civil society · Policy advice · Think tanks

Andrew Carnegie founded the Carnegie Endowment for International Peace at a critical, historic juncture. In 1910, the foundations of the system of international order that had prevailed in the nineteenth century were beginning to crack. Catastrophic war and disorder loomed. The last great surge of the Industrial Revolution was transforming the global economy.

The world is once again at a transformative moment—defined by cataclysmic threats and unimaginable opportunities. Even beyond the terrible human economic impacts of the coronavirus pandemic, profound forces

W. Burns (✉)
Carnegie Endowment for International Peace,
Washington, DC, USA

J. McGann, *The Future of Think Tanks and Policy Advice in the United States*, https://doi.org/10.1007/978-3-030-60386-1_12

are shaking the underpinning of international order: the return of great power competition; a new technological revolution that is upending how we live, work, and fight; a shift in the world's economic and military center of gravity from West to East; and growing tensions between open and closed societies, with nationalism and authoritarianism resurgent. Walls are going up faster than they are coming down. Democracy's march has slowed, even reversed, and the promise of international law and cooperation is withering on the vine. The tailwinds of globalization have transformed into powerful headwinds, and trendlines once again seem headed toward massively destabilizing collisions.

Like the international landscape itself, the marketplace of ideas is more diffuse, crowded, competitive, and contested than ever before. In the United States alone, the number of think tanks has more than doubled in a single generation. And think tanks are no longer only a transatlantic construct—more than half the world's 7000 think tanks are outside North America and Europe. Decision-makers were once starved for information; today they are drowning in it. Where there was once a small number of trusted brokers of insight and analysis, today's policy actors now have to navigate a cacophony of voices across countless platforms, with greater skepticism than ever about their reliability, credibility, and independence. Today's policy discourse is more polarized and divisive, and civil society is under growing suspicion and scrutiny.

Piercing through the noise with insights that are trusted by decision-makers, and relevant and timely to the great tests of our time, requires think tanks to rethink their mission, strategy, business model, communications, and operations. As the competition for talent intensifies, as costs balloon, as core support funding from major foundations dwindles, as grant requirements and conditionalities mushroom, as new channels of communication proliferate, as entry barriers to joining the debate crumble, as expertise is bemoaned and facts dismissed, as attention spans shrink, as speed accelerates, and as special interests work harder to shape and co-opt institutions of influence, the old ways simply won't cut it. It's always difficult to come up with a big new idea that is actually big and new and practical. But today it seems to take a great deal more purpose, effort, discipline, creativity, and good fortune to inject that idea productively into the arena.

But even as we adapt to new realities, it's even more important to demonstrate a genuine commitment to the core values that ought to animate our institutions—to independence at a time of hyperpolarization; to rigorous, high-quality scholarship at a time when punditry is drowning out serious public discourse; and to diverse perspectives beyond tired and inbred political, geographic, and disciplinary bubbles.

Having spent more than three decades as a consumer of think tank work, and now five years as a producer, I have a healthy sense of what impacts policy—and what doesn't. It's not hard to generate a lot of heat. It's much more difficult to generate light. As governments' monopolies on power, access, and influence shrink, experts sometimes make the mistake of trying to fill the void vicariously. The objective of think tanks is not to try to replicate what policymakers do—but to try to offer what they often struggle to find: views that counter conventional wisdom, perspectives embedded in local realities, that look beyond the policy horizon and help anticipate emerging challenges and opportunities, and big ideas that stretch the imagination of policymakers and challenge institutions of all stripes to cross often self-inflicted and illusory limits on the possible.

This is not a time for navel-gazing and self-flagellation about the demise of think tanks. This is not a moment to delude ourselves that we can go back to the world as we imagined it once was—full of resources, relevance, respect, and reach into the inner sanctums of power. This is not the time to decouple ourselves from parts of the world that don't share our nostalgia for the old order and all the good that flowed from it. It is also not a moment to chase after the latest fad to capture the marginal digital bandwidth or grab the latest headline.

Instead, this is the time to take a deep breath, return to first principles, and meet this moment of testing head on. We have to recognize and rectify our occasional missteps—from eroding guardrails between donors and researchers to pontificating about issues on which we have no authority to opine; from failing to hold ourselves to account for flawed analysis and failed ideas to dismissing or overlooking voices from other parts of our society that are disenchanted with the Washington consensus. We have to—at long last—come to grips with the inexcusable underrepresentation of women and minority voices in all of our work and the insufficient investment in the next generation of policy thinkers and practitioners. And we need to bury any sense of entitlement and prove that we have something valuable to offer at this moment of reckoning for our institutions and for the world in which we work.

There is an insatiable thirst for frameworks to navigate today's complex international landscape and ideas to illuminate pathways to shared peace and prosperity. We have the opportunity—and responsibility—to satiate that thirst. I'm confident that think tanks can rise to the challenge, and hopeful that institutions like Carnegie can make as big a contribution in this century as we did in the last.

Fighting for Progress in the Age of Disruption

Neera Tanden

Abstract Neera Tanden, President of The Center for American Progress Washington, DC, explores the Future of Think Tanks and Policy Advice in the United States.

Keywords Disinformation campaigns · Policy advice · Public health crisis · Think tanks

We are living through an extraordinary age of disruption. The spread of the Internet has completely transformed how we consume information, with two out of three American adults now finding most of their news on social media (Vick 2018). At the same time, our collective politics have been rapidly changed by the rise of authoritarianism and xenophobic populism. Many leaders of these recent anti-liberal movements, who view impartial facts as the tools of the opposition, have declared an all-out assault against the objective truth. These attacks have been further fueled both by hostile foreign actors looking to undermine our society through online disinformation campaigns—and by a President who has labeled

N. Tanden (✉)
Center for American Progress, Washington, DC, USA

the media as an "enemy of the people," disparaging any inconvenient reporting with the smear of "fake news."

In this environment, many may ask whether think tanks—where facts and evidence serve as the coin of the realm—are still relevant. But at this moment, our institutions are needed more than ever before. The truth must be defended—and it can still sway the public.

We saw this unfold firsthand in 2017 during the debate about repealing the Affordable Care Act. Throughout that process, the Trump administration claimed that not a single person would lose coverage (Mangan 2017b). However, the Congressional Budget Office and a myriad of other experts found that repealing the legislation would leave more than 20 million people without health insurance (Mangan 2017a).

In an era of growing popular distrust toward our public institutions and long-established sources of knowledge, we currently have an invaluable opportunity to connect directly with the people and to help restore faith in our government. Our society stands at a crossroads—and think tanks can play a meaningful role in safeguarding democratic values, both now and well into the future.

The Center for American Progress (CAP)—and our sister advocacy organization, the Center for American Progress Action Fund—were founded in 2003 to provide ideas, data, and analysis for progressive policies. Under the traditional model for how think tanks operated, the primary goal of our organization was to influence the influencers who occupied the White House and Capitol Hill. Indeed, during the first 13 years of our existence, we helped the progressive movement to realize a series of major victories by advancing bold solutions—including our efforts to develop and pass the Affordable Care Act.

To be sure, a large part of our team continues to carry out this vitally important work. However, I'm proud of the extensive steps we have taken since the start of the Trump administration in pivoting toward new strategies that are shaping our nation's growth. Those strategies include developing an effective, alternative policy agenda, engaging with officials on the state and local levels to stimulate meaningful change, and developing a robust and far-reaching digital strategy to engage and energize the American people.

From the beginning of the Trump administration, we have sought to harness the massive popular resistance against this President into concrete action to stymie his policy agenda. As a result, we have dramatically expanded our engagement with mass democracy by making greater invest-ments in digital outreach and communications. We are supporting those at the grassroots level by sharing our evidence and information, and by helping them connect to the debates happening in Washington.

By strengthening the role of these activists in shaping our laws and our conversations, we recognize that influencing the influencers is no longer enough. True change must come from directly engaging with the public as well.

For example, during the administration's relentless attempts to repeal the Affordable Care Act, our organization served on the frontlines of the effort to save the law. We produced rapid response analytics that documented the number of Americans—on both a state-by-state and a Congressional district-by-district level—who would have lost their insur-ance if the ACA had been repealed. We also launched a website that laid out the stakes in personal terms by collecting more than 5,000 testi-monials about the positive impact the ACA had made on people's lives. In total, CAP and CAP Action's campaign helped produce more than 5 million pro-ACA tweets and tens of thousands of phone calls to various elected officials, along with significant numbers of online videos and local media clips in swing states.

Since then, we have taken the lessons learned from this fight and applied them toward opposing Trump's agenda across the board. We are using in-depth analysis to expose the 2017 GOP tax bill as little more than a giveaway to large corporations and the ultra-wealthy, and to docu-ment Trump's broken promises about rebalancing the economy on behalf of working- and middle-class Americans. In addition, we are conducting focus groups in communities throughout the nation to hear their most pressing concerns about the state of our country. During these conversa-tions, we have found that people are hungry for sources of information that they can trust, and for our government to take daring action that can improve their lives. And at no point has that hunger been more apparent than during the coronavirus pandemic.

I am writing this piece in April 2020, as our country remains in the throes of the greatest public health crisis of our time. We have witnessed a federal response that has left our states under-supported, our health care system underfunded, and our people underserved. The number of cases keeps increasing and, as a result, so does the number of preventable deaths. In keeping with our strategy to engage the public, CAP has produced a roadmap outlining a safe and effective strategy to overcome this crisis, deployed rapid response data to show how the federal government has failed to adequately combat this virus in comparison to other countries, and highlighted many stories of those who have been hardest hit by this virus. By late April 2020, CAP had produced over 130 written pieces, with views trending toward one million, and CAP Action had produced 70 products, including videos and other content, totaling over 31 million views.

At CAP and CAP Action, we understand that resisting Trump is only part of the solution. To truly be successful we must look beyond his presidency and set forth a positive and affirmative vision that stands as an alternative to everything he represents. That includes developing bold plans to help the United States finally achieve landmarks such as universal health care (Center for American Progress 2019a) and a 100% clean future (Center for American Progress 2019b). It also means building on the successful outreach and engagement techniques we have deployed in standing up for the ACA and tackling the coronavirus pandemic. It means having a facts-first approach, one that energizes people across America to champion a progressive outlook no matter the challenges we may face.

Our generation has a critical choice in how we respond to this age of disruption. We have seen globalization disrupt our previously established economic order. We have seen the Internet and social media disrupt how we access information. We have seen a pandemic disrupt our health care system. And we have seen leaders such as Donald Trump completely disrupt our political system.

We are bound to face more periods of disruption in the future. To counteract them, we must develop and enact political solutions that are bold, yet also real and effective. We must pay close attention to the demands of the American people, issue a sweeping new agenda to address them, and communicate these policies directly to the public. And we must always stand behind facts and evidence. That is the way forward for think tanks.

REFERENCES

SUBMISSIONS

Center for American Progress. 2019a. RELEASE: Medicare Extra Would Provide Universal Coverage and Lower Costs for All for $2.8 Trillion.

https://www.americanprogress.org/press/release/2019/07/23/472497/release-medicare-extra-provide-universal-coverage-lower-costs-2-8-trillion/.

Hananel, Sam. Center for American Progress. 2019b. RELEASE: CAP Issues Framework for 100 Percent Clean Future by 2050. https://www.americanprogress.org/press/release/2019/10/10/475656/release-cap-issues-framework-100-percent-clean-future-2050/.

Mangan, Dan. 2017a. 24 Million Would Lose Health Insurance Coverage by 2026 Under GOP's Obamacare Replacement, New Estimate Says. CNBC. https://www.cnbc.com/2017/03/13/cbo-says-millions-lose-health-insurance-under-gop-obamacare-replacement.html.

Mangan, Dan. 2017b. Trump Advisor Conway Says No One Will Lose Health Coverage After Obamacare Repeal. CNBC. https://www.cnbc.com/2017/01/03/trump-adviser-conway-says-no-one-will-lose-health-coverage-after-obamacare-repeal.html.

Vick, Karl. 24 December 2018, & 31 December 2018. Person of the Year 2018. *Time.* https://time.com/person-of-the-year-2018-the-guardians/.

International Development Cooperation into the Decade Ahead

Masood Ahmed

Abstract Masood Ahmed, President of the Center for Global Development, Washington, DC, explores the Future of Think Tanks and Policy Advice in the United States.

Keywords Civil society · Multilateral organizations · Policy advice · Think tanks

INTRODUCTION

International development has known many successes. In the last fifty years, more people have been lifted out of poverty than ever before in the history of the world. Life expectancy, reduced infant mortality, school attendance, and other indicators of human welfare have shown extraordinary gains across much of the world.

And yet, the COVID-19 pandemic is also a stark reminder of the downside risks that come from our highly interconnected world. Prosperity and security in any part of the world is at risk when other parts are in crisis. Before COVID-19 hit us, experts were sounding a similar alarm

M. Ahmed (✉)
Center for Global Development, Washington, DC, USA

about climate change. Others were pointing to the growing list of countries where failed governments and extremist movements had combined to generate insecurity and terrorism, not only for the local population, but for their neighbors and beyond. International refugees now stand at their highest number and they remain refugees, on average, for over a decade.

Globalization and the integration of poor countries into the world economy have been key drivers of development progress, but these forces have also exacerbated inequality and alienation within countries and exposed us more directly to global problems. Polarization within societies, and the backlash against globalization, risks recent development gains and weakens efforts to achieve the shared 2030 Sustainable Development Goals.

During this period, it is all the more important that national and international policies are guided by evidence and based on sound analysis. And yet, political pressures within governments and institutional inertia in large international organizations often take precedence in shaping development programs.

Independent think tanks have been, and must remain into the future, the place for conducting research, following the data, and presenting findings to policymakers for better informed decision-making. They develop ideas based on sound research and then help to turn those ideas into practical policy solutions. And our relationships with, and reputation among, decision-makers become key; amidst a growing breakdown in trust in government and multilateral organizations by the public and the growing polarization of society, think tanks must help policymakers "be better."

Over the next decade, many forces will shape international development cooperation.

1. We will need to move from a generalized focus on poverty reduction to a recognition that the remaining poor and vulnerable in the world face specific difficulties and need targeted solutions. But we need to avoid the risks of narrow actions that only achieve some goals at the expense of other valuable outcomes, all while being cognizant of the millions of people who will fall back into poverty because of the COVID-19 pandemic. A daunting challenge to be sure.
2. As the current pandemic shows, countries and institutions need to find more effective ways to address major global challenges. The current international system for dealing with these challenges is not

up to the job in the face of future pandemics, climate change and major loss of biodiversity, and a record number of displaced persons worldwide.

3. The nongovernmental sector, private business, civil society, and tech companies need to be integrated into mainstream development thinking, which is still too heavily centered on government-to-government cooperation.

4. Climate change has, of course, become the defining long-term global challenge of our time, with China and the United States alone contributing to more than 40% of global greenhouse gas emissions. International development institutions must find sustainable development solutions that mitigate and minimize the effects of climate change on the poor.

5. The political context in which development actors operate is also changing. We have moved into a period of increasing rivalry between the United States and China. Taking stock of the US–China relationship and the litany of bilateral issues that exist today, it's easy to envision some of the most important matters that will require cooperation for years to come: intellectual property and digital privacy, maritime security, national sovereignty, and reciprocal trade to name a few. I argue development can and must be on that list, too. But I have concerns about it becoming a pawn in a new Cold War of these great power rivals. That would benefit no one.

The International System and CGD's Role

In fact, I venture that it is the rules-based international system that has contributed to development progress to date, and how we will face down the COVID-19 pandemic while also moving forward on the SDGs and climate change. International finance institutions and multilateral development banks, and organizations like the United Nations and World Trade Organization, have a vital role to play in maintaining a rules-based order for future development. The future success of low- and middle-income countries—those nations which development policy and practice are intended to help most—hinges on such an order. The question is, will these organizations be relatively safe spaces to facilitate it—or will they be sorted into friends and foes in Washington and Beijing's game, where aid becomes more an instrument of loyalty rather than a promotion of anti-poverty and pro-growth health, economic, and finance programs. How can these international organizations step up and shape the space? And what can think tanks do to help them modernize and create wider-ranging but more equitable policies?

CGD and others can start making recommendations now on the post-crisis architecture and rules-based system that will be needed in the years to come. In response to the COVID-19 pandemic, multilateral banks are being called upon to provide large, unprecedented amounts of financing to a historic number of countries. In the future, as countries need more money to deal with future pandemics, climate change, and conflict and fragility, their needs may be greater than the institutions can bear with their current constraints. For example, our recommendation of the Global Health Security Challenge Fund was an attempt to put a sound idea out into the ether for debate and analysis for G7 leadership action (Glassman 2020).

Think tanks like CGD, which are not swayed by partisanship and are driven by data, can help international organizations and financial institutions think differently and outside of their natural limitations. CGD can bring realism to these complex situations. From running the numbers on the levels of financing multilateral banks can provide, to shedding light on the realities of blended finance and private sector engagement, or WHO rules, mission, and limitations, CGD can shift conversations from aspirations to achievable policy.

CONCLUSION

CGD's founder, Ed Scott, declared at our outset that we would not be a sandbox for economists and experts to play in and talk among ourselves. From our niche corner, we've worked diligently the last 20 years to rigorously follow the evidence, analyze and make recommendations to policymakers, and constantly convene the multi sectoral development world around ideas that work.

The impacts of food and water shortages, global climate change, pandemics, and resource-driven conflicts disproportionately fall on poor people the world over. And these challenges are only going to increase and intensify in the decades to come. COVID-19 has shown us that the development community needs to understand these challenges and be proactive in responding to looming crises. Nonpartisan and data-driven experts, like those at CGD and other think tanks, are critical to informed decision-making on effective development.

The original objectives we set for development at the turn of the century have been superseded by the new SDGs, known and unknown pandemics, and unmitigated climate change. What does this mean for the future of development cooperation? In the coming years, the challenge for think tanks like CGD and our contemporaries will be adapting a substantive, solutions-oriented workstream for policymakers to address this new global agenda.

Reference

Submission

Glassman, Amanda. 10 March 2020. The Call for a Global Health Security Challenge Fund. Center for Global Development. https://www.cgdev.org/blog/call-global-health-security-challenge-fund.

Think Tanks in the New Century

John Hamre

Abstract John Hamre, President and CEO of the Center for Strategic and International Studies, Washington, DC, explores the Future of Think Tanks and Policy Advice in the United States.

Keywords Policy advice · Think tanks

Think tanks in America emerged about a hundred years ago. Prior to that time, the primary source of policy research and innovation was limited, coming largely from entities with parochial interests. During the past fifty years, the policy ideas industry has expanded dramatically. While representing only a fraction of an ecosystem of wider ideas, think tanks have become a far more prominent feature on the Washington policy landscape. This essay discusses the growing role and significance of think tanks within the policy ecosystem. Broadly speaking, the ideas industry includes universities, trade associations, professional associations, lobbying organizations (both profit-seeking and nonprofit), corporate offices, law firms, news media outlets, and think tanks. I will first set an important reference point before I discuss the role and future of think tanks.

J. Hamre (✉)
Center for Strategic and International Studies, Washington, DC, USA

103

J. McGann, *The Future of Think Tanks and Policy Advice
in the United States*, https://doi.org/10.1007/978-3-030-60386-1_15

Every country and every society has the same problem. How does the government understand the significance of new developments—technology developments, business initiatives, social changes, etc.—and adapt its policies to exploit the positive potential or mitigate the negative consequences of these developments? Most countries in the world use their universities for this purpose. In the United States, all the various actors in the ideas industry play a role in midwifing new policies. During the last fifty years, universities have receded from this role, except in the physical and life sciences. Think tanks have significantly replaced the historic role that universities once played.

There is no standard model or template for think tanks. Some think tanks embrace an ideological philosophy. Some are analytic shops while others are advocacy shops. Some champion the perspective of business, others of labor, and yet others of the environment, the oceans or other focused interests. But all of them share a common purpose— to understand the significance of important changes in the world, how government policy is affected by those changes, and what should be done about it.

It is important to note a critical dimension that underlies the activities of think tanks and other actors in the ideas industry. The first Article of the Bill of Rights delineates fundamental rights of American citizens. The last delineated right is "to petition the government for a redress of grievances." This right is widely interpreted to be a right of citizens and entities (corporations, associations, city and state governments, etc.) to lobby for their specific interests and seek decisions by the Government that will favor those interests. Government ethics law is structured around this fundamental right. Ethics law refers to "particular matters," which is a term of art that refers to discrete interest that is unique to a petitioner. A particular matter would be something like pushing the Corps of Engineers to dredge a channel in a specific river so that shipping volumes can increase for a port on that river. The law allows individuals and organizations to lobby the government on "particular matters," but the ground rules for lobbying activity are regulated. Some elements of the ideas industry deal specifically with these particular-matter issues, notably law firms, for-profit lobbying organizations, consulting companies, etc. Generally, trade associations, professional associations, and think tanks do not lobby for particular-matter interests. Generally, these outfits lobby for "general interest" matters, defined as benefits to a class of people or entities, which are available to all citizens if they share those interests.

This is a crucial distinction, and is the most important discriminator of the role of think tanks. Think tanks have a privileged position in American society, in that they are allowed to receive tax-exempt contributions. In exchange for granting them this privilege, the Government imposes rules and regulations to govern their behavior to ensure that they work on matters of general interest. I meet with every employee who comes to CSIS, and I discuss this crucial concept. Because we have a privileged position in American society and are allowed to receive tax-deductible contributions, it is our obligation to sit on the government's side of the table. We play a critical role for the Government. We have the luxury of time and perspective to understand the critical ways that new technologies, business practices, demographic changes, etc., will change American society, and how best to capture the opportunities they present through policy innovation.

Unfortunately, the Government is losing its capacity to understand the changing world it must modulate in order to best serve the broad public interest. The pace of change is accelerating in every dimension, yet government structures remain static. Every complex problem now is "horizontal" and all government structures are "vertical." These new and complex problems have many dimensions that go beyond the jurisdictional boundaries of any one government agency. However, Government agencies attempt to deal with these issues within their previously established authorities.

This problem is amplified by three other serious challenges. The first is the structure of congressional oversight. We last had a significant reform in committee jurisdictions back in 1946–1947. Since that time committees have wrestled with jurisdictional changes on the margin. And these jurisdictional boundaries reinforce the stovepipe structures of government agencies. A perfect example is to see how hamstrung the Federal Government has been to develop new comprehensive privacy policies in an age of digital data and communications.

And add to this the second problem. Government ethics regulations have significantly narrowed the channels by which the private sector can talk with the Government. It is still open for lobbying the congress, but the channels to engage executive branch agencies is found now almost entirely in the layer of political appointees. The average assistant secretary of something usually serves only 22–26 months. That is far too little time to understand the complex operations of her or his organization, let alone to chart sustainable policy changes. Most assistant secretaries are champions for the bureaucratic interests of their respective little plantations and not the whole of the department, much less the whole of government, when problems are becoming more complicated and multidimensional.

The third problem concerns the civil service. We have crippled this crucial element of government by creating a politically driven atmosphere of condescension directed against the civil service. I had the privilege of working directly with talented civil servants in the Department of Defense for nearly eight years. They were talented and hard-working, but struggled to do their best within antiquated business systems and rigid bureaucratic boundaries. Ethics regulations are seriously limiting the interaction between civil servants and private sector actors.

All of this is the context to understand the crucial role that think tanks now play in the American policy landscape. Scholars in think tanks have the freedom to talk openly with people in both governmental and private sector offices. We have the capacity (and I would argue the obligation) to create open forums where the governed and the government can meet outside of rigid regulatory venues. We have a unique capacity to understand the interests and needs of both the government and the private sector, and to craft policy alternatives for deliberation.

Again, it is crucial to emphasize that any honest think tank sits on the government's side of the table in these matters. It is our role and obligation to understand the broad public interest that is inherent in the face of changing technologies, business models, economic and demographic changes. It is our role and obligation to identify alternative policy choices that can address these developments, to enhance the benefit broadly to American society and to mitigate the adverse consequences of developments that are not adequately addressed within existing policy frameworks. We are not encumbered by the rigidities of agency authorities or committee jurisdictions.

I meet with every incoming employee at CSIS to emphasize our obligations as an institution and our approach to solving problems. Our government is slow-moving and rigid. Politics is limiting experimentation. Innovation is small and on the margins of long-established mandates and paradigms. We have never had a time when think tanks were more important for America's progress. Fortunately, I see an honest understanding in both legislative and executive branch offices of the importance of this critical role that we play. The importance of think tanks in America is growing. It is our obligation to meet this growing need and to do so in a way that reinforces our credibility as objective, transparent, and effective policy innovators.

Bridging Policy Needs with Technology Solutions

Brian Finlay and James Siebens

Abstract Brian Finlay, President and James Siebens, Fellow at the Stimson Center, Washington, DC, explores the Future of Think Tanks and Policy Advice in the United States.

Keywords Disinformation campaigns · Policy advice · Policy community · Policy experts · Think tanks · Transparency

Remarkable advances in communications technology over the past two decades have radically transformed public access to information on a global scale. They have diluted the traditional power enjoyed by governments and a handful of mass media outlets to shape and influence public perceptions. The results of this trend have been a mixture of both mass empowerment and mass confusion. Even as the proliferation of information sources has democratized public narratives and energized political debates, it has likewise contributed to political polarization, eviscerated

B. Finlay (✉) · J. Siebens
Henry L. Stimson Center, Washington, DC, USA

public trust in expertise and institutions, enabled widespread disinformation campaigns, and fostered the development of outlets which reinforce the preconceptions of their audiences.

In this contentious marketplace, think tanks must attempt to serve the public interest at a time of intense domestic political division, unprecedented policy complexity, and renewed tensions between the world's great powers. At the very moment in which our role in educating policymakers and the public has become more important than ever, public receptivity to expert analysis and opinion is at an all-time low. This dual crisis of public perception and political strife highlights the need for think tanks to eschew partisan talking points and rather focus on utilizing tools and research methods that bolster the credibility of our research and analysis. This means engaging new stakeholders in shaping the future of public policy and communicating information and analysis to politically diverse audiences in ways that are both innovative and impactful.

Fortuitously, even as technological advancement presents new challenges to the think tank community, it equally provides new opportunities to marry our solutions to global problems in order to have real-world impact. There can be little doubt that the methodical pace of problem-solving by the policy community is at fundamental odds with: (1) the fevered pace of technology innovation and (2) the public interest in policy. Bridging the divide between global problems and technology-oriented solutions therefore necessitates reasoned brokers to negotiate between these two equally important communities.

Unfortunately, for many in the tech sector, engagement with think tanks and the policy community more generally, is often viewed with consternation. For the fast-paced world of tech, the think tank sector is too old, too tired, too captured by staid bureaucratic interests, and too slow. For our part, the think tank community has too often viewed the tech community as earnest outsiders or convenient ATMs rather than as practical partners in developing and implementing solutions to grand challenges. Further, the technology community is often hampered by a lack of practical policy and political experience. Just as thinking "outside the Beltway" is difficult, so has thinking "outside the Bay Area" proven to be a challenge for many in high-tech industries. Witness the unintended consequences of technological innovation for national security and democracy, as illustrated by recent debates around the responsibility of social media firms to the public interest. Righting this relationship must be a high priority across both of our communities.

Stimson has sought to engage with the world of tech in new ways by launching the Alfred Lee Loomis Innovation Council, a group of technology experts and entrepreneurs who regularly convene with Stimson's policy experts. The goal of the council is to not only wed policy expertise with innovations from industry but also to equip tech industry leaders with a better understanding of the policymaking process. The Council's ambitious goal is to address some of the world's most complex policy challenges with replicable and scalable solutions informed by leaders drawn from a variety of high-tech enterprises. Experts present problems with the potential for technology interventions, and Loomis Council members contribute their diverse networks, expertise, and experience to help identify and craft practical solutions. In turn, the tech community gains insight into the global challenges facing millions of people and scores of governments around the world, thus creating productive new partnerships between people interested in solving big problems. The result is one of the most creative and constructive cultures in the world of think tanks.

To date, Stimson has undertaken a number of projects that leverage advancements in data analysis tools and techniques, online resources, and new sources of information, such as satellite imagery and geographic information systems (GIS) (Stimson Center). These tools give us the ability to produce data-driven analyses of diverse public policy and international security challenges, ranging from nuclear crises to the overexploitation of natural resources, to illegal trade and trafficking.

By way of example, Stimson's "38 North" online journal pioneered the use of commercial satellite imagery to track and monitor developments at North Korea's key nuclear and ballistic missile facilities. Our analysis yields timely information about how these programs may be progressing in an otherwise opaque environment, helping also to hold governments accountable for the veracity of their claims about the security situation on the Korean Peninsula. Stimson is thus able to provide a public oversight function in one of the world's most tense, high-stakes security situations by using insights from technology that were previously available only to intelligence services and corporations.

Likewise, Stimson is using data collected from ship transponders to track vessel movements, such as maritime Automatic Identification Systems (AIS) and Vessel Monitoring Systems (VMS), to identify and analyze the activities of distant water fishing fleets. This data-driven approach has enabled us to better understand the scale and patterns of distant water fishing operations—both legal and illicit—and quantify the scale of their impact on local economies and global security. Our work has shed new light on this under-appreciated area of international security, with clear implications for global food markets, environmental degradation, economic security of coastal nations, and international competition for scarce resources. It has also inspired legislative and multilateral action to ameliorate the harmful impact of distant water fishing on fisheries and the communities that depend on them.

As part of our ongoing effort to reduce the risk of conflict escalation and nuclear dangers on the Subcontinent, Stimson has created an open online course, "Nuclear South Asia." The course aims to stimulate fresh thinking and debate on nuclear deterrence, competition, and crises among the next generation of strategists and policymakers in India and Pakistan. By offering the course, which integrates both theoretical foundations and diverse expertise to students, university professors, and policymakers via a free online educational platform, Stimson is helping to enrich strategic analysis in South Asia. We have also begun to use machine learning to better understand strategic discourse and thinking across the Subcontinent. This approach promises to challenge status-quo thinking and yield new, empirically grounded research on how regional strategic communities conceptualize deterrence, arms control, and nuclear risk, and provide clarity to better-suited policy responses.

Stimson is also engaging directly in novel applications of new technologies across the globe. Our "Blockchain in Practice" initiative seeks to identify and develop real-world applications of distributed ledger technology (DLT) like blockchain in the fields of nuclear security, safeguards information management, export controls, and the control of dual-use chemical precursors. Our experts are on the leading edge of developing and testing use-cases for augmenting existing security frameworks for tracking and controlling chemical, biological, radiological and nuclear materials using DLT. This year, our experts began work on a prototype DLT-based system of state control for nuclear materials. Our work to leverage the unprecedented transparency, traceability, and reliability made possible through DLT for use in controlling some of the world's most dangerous items promises to transform the world of nonproliferation and trade security.

The generation of knowledge for the sake of knowledge will always be essential; however, in our view, the role of a modern think tank is to transform these new ideas into policy solutions. By leveraging technology in innovative ways, and by providing an onramp for the tech sector to contribute to global problem-solving, the think tank community can help regain the trust of those constituencies we seek to influence. In short, the think tank community has a unique opportunity to learn by doing—brokering new opportunities for the application of some of the same technologies that threaten our relevance for the pursuit of good policy solutions.

The size, scope, and complexity of today's global issues means that there is little time to lament the negative impacts that technology has had on the approaches of yesterday. Unless our sector embraces technological advancement and actively helps to redirect it in service of the public interest, the think tank community will rightly recede into irrelevance.

America's Think Tanks: Meeting the Challenges of Increasing Competition and New Technologies, and Maintaining Relevance in an Ever-Changing World

Kay Coles James

Abstract Kay Coles James, President of The Heritage Foundation in Washington, DC, explores the history, evolution and future of think tanks Future of Think Tanks and Policy Advice in the United States.

Keywords Policy advice · Think tanks

Over the years, US. think tanks have played a vital role in providing policymakers at the local, state, and federal levels with detailed research and policy recommendations to create more informed and data-centered solutions for the issues facing America.

As think tanks look to the future, we must be committed to both preservation and progress—maintaining the strengths of original research and independence while developing new ways to meet the challenges

K. C. James (✉)
The Heritage Foundation, Washington, DC, USA

© The Author(s) 2021   115
J. McGann, *The Future of Think Tanks and Policy Advice in the United States*, https://doi.org/10.1007/978-3-030-60386-1_17

of increased competition, new technologies, finding new donors, and maintaining relevance in an ever-changing world.

This essay explores some of the challenges that think tanks currently face and will continue to encounter, including how technology has impacted the work of think tanks, how new competitors like law firms and advocacy groups have transformed the public policy landscape, and how increased political polarization has changed the nature of policy advice. We will also examine how think tanks can meet their recruiting challenges, how funding impacts the independence of research, and the value we provide in a highly competitive marketplace of ideas.

The Impact of Technology

The wealth of data collected by governments, social media companies, and other entities gives researchers access to a tremendous amount of information about our world. Moreover, the ease with which data can be used in its digital form also means that researchers can cross-reference it with lots of other data to show patterns and draw conclusions at a pace and quantity we hadn't previously imagined. Technology not only allows us to more selectively target with whom we communicate, but also allows us to effectively tailor our message to particular audiences, whether that is policymakers, the media, donors, or the general public.

Technology also helps us deliver our messages in more compelling and persuasive ways. No longer is a white paper sufficient for reaching a mass audience. Videos, graphics, and emotive stories combined with policy research and disseminated through traditional media, social media, and the Internet are more effective ways to reach audiences.

In the area of donor development, technology allows think tanks to accumulate and analyze information about how donors give, the media they consume, how they prefer to communicate, their passions, and so on. This information can be fed into predictive modeling software to assign individual donors to particular solicitation tracks such as monthly giver, annual giver, planned giver, or major donor—and help predict the most effective ways to grow individual relationships with them.

New Competitors

Newer competitors such as law firms, advocacy groups, nontraditional media sources, and even online search engines have transformed the public policy landscape, but of course, not all information sources are equal.

Think tank research must set itself apart by being seen as more credible, reliable, and independent. While advocacy groups, public relations firms, and others may have email lists and Twitter followers, they don't have the data and the research that think tanks do. In some cases, authors intentionally try to disguise advocacy as fact. In other instances, research that's not checked by a rigorous review process can lead to unsupported conclusions and poor policy advice. This is an area where think tanks can better assure audiences of the accuracy of the data and the neutrality of the conclusions derived from it.

Often though, we may find that other entities that are seeking to influence policy aren't actually competitors. Many times, they can play the role of coalition partners or third-party validators. It is important to understand their motivations and goals. Where there's common ground, there may also be important opportunities to work together.

Increased Political Polarization

The increasing polarization of politics and fragmentation of Americans have dramatically changed the nature of public discourse and policy advising. In the past, lawmakers from both sides of the aisle would embrace certain policy ideas that were sound, regardless of the ideological leanings of the think tank presenting them.

Today, many elected leaders appear less interested in actual data and instead seem more inclined to embrace hardened political positions. This has limited the ability of those think tanks that are seen as having more in common with "the other side" to work across partisan lines.

One way to counter this is to communicate directly to the public in order to build the bipartisan support needed to encourage elected officials to adopt our policies. Engaging the public with policy ideas in plain language and convincing them to buy in is often key to winning legislative support. That's not how think tanks have often operated, but it's the reality we encounter when it comes to moving policymakers to action.

The key to getting past the partisanship with the public is to talk about issues from common ground. Most average citizens, whether liberal, moderate, or conservative, care about clean air and water, helping the poor, creating jobs, and ensuring no one goes without needed health care. They just see different ways of achieving those goals.

In that regard, think tanks need to do what think tanks do best: assess honestly where both history and the data show that certain policies have failed and may have even hurt the people they were intended to help. We then must consider solutions that science, economics, and other social sciences point to as producing the outcomes we seek while also protecting the freedom, prosperity, and the rights of the individual that have defined America from the start.

Then, when engaging with the public, think tanks must communicate in ways that appeal first to the heart, which leads to engagement of the mind. To be done effectively, this often involves conducting market research to determine where to reach audiences (the media, social media, and other communication forms they use) and the best language to communicate our ideas clearly and compellingly.

HUMAN RESOURCE CHALLENGES

Think tanks have always faced recruiting challenges, whether competing with governments, other think tanks, or the private sector for talent. To expand their candidate pools, organizations have been expanding their social media and job board advertising, and others have hired recruiters.

A key talent pipeline is internship programs. At The Heritage Foundation, for example, one in five employees was once a Heritage intern. To grow their intern programs, think tanks should expand outreach efforts on college campuses through job fairs and other venues to attract more applicants.

To continue attracting and retaining quality employees, think tanks will also need to look at more creative or generous benefits programs to keep up with other employers. This includes offering telecommuting, which is an attractive option where employees may accept a less competitive salary in exchange for the ability to work from home.

Additionally, to ensure a think tank's impact continues beyond the tenure of a single CEO, vice president, or star scholar, they must also create succession plans to build a bench of talent capable of seamlessly continuing the mission of the organization. At Heritage, we sought advice from a corporate ally about the process. It was simple enough: our senior managers identified their positions' core competencies, they identified two or three internal candidates who could best replace them, and they are working on getting the candidates the necessary training to prepare them for those roles.

Funding

When think tanks diversify their income streams, they lessen their dependence on large donors. This increases their ability to tout their research independence and helps ensure they won't have to close their doors or lay off employees if they lose a major donor. Diversification also provides protection from economic downturns, as small-dollar donations, planned gifts, and endowments are generally less affected than major gifts.

One of the lesser used, but still important areas of revenue diversification include creating membership programs where average citizens can support a think tank with a small annual donation. Membership programs and small-dollar automatic monthly giving programs have a dramatic impact on lifetime giving from individuals. They also serve as a pipeline for developing major donors: when you can regularly communicate to your members the successes that result from their donations, trust, affinity, and contributions grow over time.

The Value Add of Think Tanks

Think tanks must do a better job communicating how they provide added value in a highly competitive, information-rich marketplace of ideas.

They must tout the fact that they provide accurate and thorough original research that others cannot. They must critically point out the flaws of bad ideas, avoid ad hominem attacks, and show the facts to back up their own ideas. They must maintain their unparalleled level of scholarship and independence—it's what separates serious think tanks from the talking heads on TV and Twitter stars who speak loudly but without authority.

To maintain their credibility, think tanks must also adhere to a transparent set of principles so they can be consistent in their recommendations across policies and across time, and so policymakers and the public know the foundation upon which their solutions are based. At Heritage, we've found that our 14 published "True North" principles help us in managing our audiences' expectations and provide them an understanding of why we stand on one side of an issue versus the other.

As the government becomes more intrusive in our daily lives, as politics becomes more polarized, as misleading information becomes more abundant in the marketplace of ideas, and as policymakers and the American public look more skeptically at the news media and social media as biased sources of information, think tanks can have an even greater impact in the debate over public policy, serving as the fact-based, unbiased truth-tellers that people can turn to for honest solutions to address the most pressing issues of the day.

In doing so, think tanks aren't just the problem solvers, but they can also become the uniters that this country so desperately needs.

Addendum: The Impact of COVID-19 on Think Tanks and Policy Advice

The worldwide impact of the 2020 COVID-19 pandemic created new challenges for the think tank world. It showed us that if we didn't already have them in place, we needed to create disaster plans to ensure our continued operations during any disaster—especially during a case where local, state, and federal governments relied on our expertise to help navigate the nation through the crisis and toward recovery.

The coronavirus crisis also demonstrated the importance of having significant financial reserves to weather a storm big enough to cause a virtual economic shutdown. It showed the importance of diversifying our donor bases with small donors who were more likely to keep donating even when economic crises hit, as well as large donors who had the ability to add an extra zero to their contributions to help make up for the loss of revenue elsewhere.

The crisis demonstrated the need to maintain ongoing communications with policymakers, the media, and donors through the use of videoconferencing, tele-town halls, and webinars, as well as what types of things we should communicate: what part, if any, our organizations were playing in solving the crisis; the solutions we proposed; what resources we needed from our supporters to accomplish those things; and reassurances that our organizations were weathering the storm and continuing our critical work.

The coronavirus pandemic also sounded the clarion call that we needed to have the technology, capacity, and IT support in place to ensure that part or all of our workforce could still do their jobs via telecommuting. Governments would need our advice during this and future crises. Think tank experts were needed to analyze legislation and policies being considered. And at a time when most policymakers felt the need to support almost anything that seemed like a solution, and others responded with measures that threatened our freedoms, and still others slipped in unrelated amendments to benefit certain constituencies, the nation needed its think tanks to alert them to the pitfalls and unintended consequences of legislation that was being rushed through.

Finally, the crisis reminded us that, working together, our think tanks covered the broad range of expertise that was needed to combat and recover from the pandemic. We could find new ways to come together, share our knowledge, and collaborate on vital solutions that would ultimately bring the American people through the crisis and leave us even stronger than we were before.

Reflections on the Future of Think Tanks, Drawing on Three Decades in Public Policy Research

Kenneth R. Weinstein

Abstract Kenneth R. Weinstein, President and CEO of The Hudson Institute in Washington, DC, explores the Future of Think Tanks and Policy Advice in the United States.

Keywords Fundraising · Ivory tower · Policy advice · Policy analysis · Policy research organization · Think tanks

My three decades in public policy research have seen the think tank landscape deeply transformed. Some of these changes reflect the world around us, including some in policy research organizations that helped bring about: the fall of the Soviet Union, the rise of automation, the communications revolution including the rise of the Internet and social media. Other changes are more specific to think tank business models: an increasing focus on events, less long-term and original work, larger budgets and endowments, and evermore upscale institutional facilities.

K. R. Weinstein (✉)
The Hudson Institute, Washington, DC, USA

J. McGann, *The Future of Think Tanks and Policy Advice in the United States*, https://doi.org/10.1007/978-3-030-60386-1_18

Some of these trends are likely to be accelerated as we move into the era of big data and artificial intelligence; others may be reversed. But, as think tanks increasingly focus on the immediate need to remain relevant to both the news cycle and legislative calendars, the need for smart, strategic, independent, and original policy research will continue to grow in an era of growing uncertainty.

One of the most striking changes over the past few decades is that think tanks have largely moved away from the "university without students" model and have far less of an "ivory tower" ethos—especially as a more nuanced understanding of the unintended consequences of abstract policy schemes has emerged. "Over-the-horizon" research and books are no longer the primary products of think tanks.

Rapid response is now increasingly valued over scholarship; a think tank scholar's op-eds and tweets to influence public opinion seem to matter far more than their books or footnotes. Likewise, in the parallel quest to shape the daily policy narrative, think tanks are increasingly events platforms, knowing that well-timed and well-choreographed panel discussions can shape headlines more efficiently than more expensive, time-consuming, and unpredictable research efforts. The Heritage Foundation pioneered this approach in the 1970s, recognizing that a dilatory approach to policy analysis led to a diminished impact on public debate—and the entire think tank universe has, to varying degrees, come to follow Heritage's lead.

Just as original research has become less valued in the think tank world, the "tooth-to-tail ratio" in the industry—the ratio of scholars to management staff—has decreased. Think tanks today deploy larger numbers of outreach staff focused on the media, government relations (including international government relations), as well as fundraising, in a competitive think tank landscape in which funders increasingly focus on the ability to move policy when deciding on institutional investments.

As major think tanks grow on the management side and build more elegant facilities, think tanks, moreover, have moved to a hybrid employment model, with fewer organizations demanding that their fellows be full-time employees. This accelerates the process whereby think tank administrators increasingly shape a think tank's agenda, rather than the "university without students" model in which scholars, by and large, had greater independence.

Funding models have also shifted significantly in the industry. Gone are the days in which my Hudson colleague Chris DeMuth, the former president of the American Enterprise Institute for a quarter century, relied upon major corporate CEOs who viewed it as their civic duty to support think tank policy research as a hands-off investment in America's future. Today, with greater scrutiny of corporate budgets, corporate support for think tanks comes from corporate public affairs, directed for specific projects or initiatives. While this funding underwrites key initiatives, it is increasingly rare that such funding comes simply to support the core mission of the organization.

Another major shift in the funding model parallels the increasingly polarized political scene. As think tanks move away from the ivory tower model, they, by and large, place themselves on a political continuum from right to left. This leads to think tanks pitching their work not just to major American foundations but to increasingly wealthy individuals of an ideological cohort. Maintaining research independence in the face of various pressures, especially related to funding, will remain a critical task for think tank administrators.

Policymakers have become an evermore important audience and constituency for think tanks and the government seems to be playing an increased role in shaping what think tanks do. Some of this is natural. Technology has a more central role in society as well as in shaping national security, bringing with it complex and often interrelated challenges that transcend traditional academic disciplines and require serious examination by, and counsel for, officials who face an array of policy options, as well as the risk of massive and unintended consequences. Following the lead of think tanks such as Brookings, the Center for New American Security, CSIS and Hudson, it is reassuring to see a wide array of think tanks across the political spectrum now focus on technological transformation as a critical dimension of geostrategic competition.

Notwithstanding the major shifts in the world of think tanks, the biggest challenge we in the think tank community face is the same challenge that the founders of Hudson Institute, Herman Kahn and Max Singer, faced when they launched Hudson in 1961: to balance the policymaker's need for immediate policy options, often tactical, with the need for longer term and strategic thinking about broader trends, policy risks, and opportunities.

Think tankers who get lost in either the media or legislative cycle without "opening the policy aperture" wider, and "expanding the policy imagination," as Kahn would have argued, risk overlooking the kinds of bold and unconventional proposals such as civil defense and missile defense that were so critical to avoiding the worst pitfalls of the Cold War. Challenging the pessimists with original, thoughtful options that stand outside the echo chamber that think tanks and the media can become, especially in the age of social media, is essential to assure a brighter future.

This is especially important with the rise of artificial intelligence as a standard research tool for think tanks in the coming years. The sheer amount of data available for analysis will expand exponentially over the next few years, as will the temptation to do frequent data runs. Framing queries broadly will be key to research that does more than merely reiterate political or policy messaging, as the questions asked will largely determine the answers received. The good news is that with increasing access to data, queries—especially shallow ones—will be subject to the kind of rapid, "fact-check" style of review.

AI is far from a "silver bullet" in determining policy options. AI will facilitate original research queries and the writing and editing of papers, but like any research tool, it will require interpretation, informed judgment, and a critical perspective to harness its massive analytic capacity to its fullest potential.

In conclusion, I would argue that think tanks have never been more prominent than they are today. And this prominence will continue over the next few decades. This is not because of the coming rise of AI, or because our budgets and endowments have grown significantly or because we have higher media profiles and the kind of state-of-the-art facilities that none of us dared dream about just a few years ago. Instead, it's because of the very visible failures of the conventional wisdom and of establishments around the globe, including think tanks: we are in a new era, both domestically and internationally, with the rise of China as a near-peer competitor, with Cold War institutions and strategies questioned and in need of major reform to meet new challenges, and with the potential transformation and threats of the Fourth Industrial Revolution looming ever closer.

Each of these challenges is long-term ones, and government policy-makers find themselves, as they did throughout the twentieth century, lacking the time and bandwidth to think originally, creatively and synoptically about emerging concepts, threats, and opportunities they may only be faintly aware of. Wise officials, knowing their limits, will increasingly turn to think tanks to learn how to think about policy challenges we cannot even begin to think about today.

Thought Leadership in Uncertain Times: Four Global Trends

Adam Lupel

Abstract Adam Lupel, Acting President and Chief Executive Officer of The International Peace Institute in New York, NY explores the Future of Think Tanks and Policy Advice in the United States.

Keywords Latin American think tanks · North American think tanks · Policy advice · Research institutions · Think tanks

We live in a time of great environmental, political, and technological change. As a result, questions concerning the shape of the future are high on many people's minds. Governments and institutions are crafting plans and determining investments based upon their assumptions about what the future holds. Think tanks, such as the International Peace Institute (IPI), are no different. We write this as the novel coronavirus, COVID-19, spreads across the globe. As of late March 2020, the outbreak is present in at least 196 countries and territories, and cases are growing exponentially. Questions about the future suddenly include a new variable of uncertainty. The social, economic, political, and security ripple effects

A. Lupel (✉)
Acting President and Chief Executive Officer, International Peace Institute, New York, NY, USA

J. McGann, *The Future of Think Tanks and Policy Advice in the United States*, https://doi.org/10.1007/978-3-030-60386-1_19

of Covid-19 will be profound. This will certainly affect the work of think tanks as well.

Already, the pandemic's impact on the global economy is apparent. It will transform the funding environment for many nonprofits. In the wake of the 2008 financial crisis, philanthropy dropped by 15 percent, and many nonprofits saw a long-term decline in core funding (Dorfman and Dorsey 2020; Kelstrup 2016: 69). Similar effects may be seen in the wake of this crisis, but for some research institutions, the opposite could be true. Those institutions that are well placed to make a positive contribution to policymaking in response to the pandemic across a variety of issue areas could see an increase in funding opportunities.

The future of think tanks will be shaped by how they navigate this new terrain. Choices being made today will have long-term consequences. However, to fully answer the questions addressed by this volume, we must consider the larger trends that began long before the current crisis. What is the future of the think tank landscape and why does it matter?

To ask about the future of think tanks is to ask in part about the future of both state and society, for the best think tanks provide a bridge between the two. The twenty-first century will be an era of extraordinary transformation. Global processes and new technologies are broadly transforming state and society, and the role of think tanks in the future will reflect those transformations.

It is, of course, notoriously risky to hazard a guess about the specificity of future events. "Prediction is very difficult," said Nils Bohr, "especially if it is about the future." But we can identify general trends that will clearly impact the world over the coming years and surmise how they may affect our work.

For the International Peace Institute, this includes a broad transition underway in the multilateral system—a moment of transition fraught with uncertainty that is only being exacerbated by the lack of global coordination around the coronavirus. IPI is different from many of the think tanks represented in this volume. While we are headquartered in the United States, our focus is not principally on providing policy advice to US institutions. We are based in New York, across the street from the United Nations, and our principal partners are the UN Secretariat and the Member State Permanent Missions to the UN.

For any think tank operating in the space of international affairs, questions regarding the decline of the liberal international order, the rise of

China, the return of populist nationalism, divisions within the North Atlantic system of collective security, and the troubled status of the United Nations are all of critical importance.

We can identify four broad, interrelated trends that provide both risks and opportunities for think tanks of all kinds:

First, of central concern to IPI, is the hardening of geopolitical divisions and the transformation of the multilateral system. If the end of the Cold War ushered in a brief period of unipolarity and a potential New World Order governed by a globalized commitment to liberal democracy and free trade, that period is clearly over and not returning any time soon. The rise of China as a global power has inspired predictions of a return to a bipolar world and a potential new Cold War, but the future will likely be more complex than that.

Multipolarity is a more likely scenario, as divisions within the West are at risk of widening; regional rivalries—for example between Iran and Saudi Arabia or India and Pakistan—continue to drive geopolitical considerations; and non-state actors, from armed groups to the corporate sector, wield increasing transnational influence. Meanwhile, Russia will continue to assert itself as an independent great power to the best of its ability. The international order will likely contain multiple, overlapping rule-bound orders, and internationally focused think tanks will have to navigate that terrain with sophistication to determine where the opportunities for influence lie and who should be the object of effective policy advice.

Second, broad economic transformations will continue to inspire historic changes in state–society relations and international affairs. As inequality within countries has risen in the post-Cold War era, inequality between countries has declined (Milanovic 2020). This is largely due to the general rebalancing of economic power from the West to the East—in particular China and India. Fast-growing economies in Africa have also been an important part of this equation, although the economic impact of the coronavirus may alter this trend in the short term.

This shift in economic power offers new opportunities for partnerships between European and North American think tanks. This includes new donor relationships, with the public and private sector, but also partnerships in knowledge production. In the future, partnerships between North American and Asian, African, or Latin American think tanks will be more common and mutually advantageous.

This does present some risks however, as many of the fastest-growing economies have authoritarian tendencies. Similarly, rising inequality within states has occasioned the resurgence of populist nationalism, instigating an inauspicious turn toward illiberal policies which could deepen in the future, especially in the wake of a global economic crisis precipitated by the coronavirus. To the extent that the funding and partnership landscape shifts increasingly toward authoritarian sources, think tanks will have to vigilantly guard their independence to maintain credibility.

Third, changes to information technology and the modes of communication will have a profound impact on all knowledge producers. In the coming years how information is packaged, how policy advice is communicated, and how input from constituents is received are all likely to go through multiple rounds of transformation. While this presents new opportunities to expand the reach and impact of think tanks, many of the challenges of the new media environment are already evident.

The media environment of the future is likely to be even more fragmented than it is already. The days when Walter Cronkite, a single anchorman on one of only three nightly news broadcasts, could be identified in an opinion poll as "the most trusted man in America" is long gone. As George Orwell already observed looking back on the Spanish Civil War, it would seem that "the very concept of objective truth is fading from the world" (McIntyre 2018). In an era of fake news, "post truth," and competitive realities, the role that think tanks play in providing evidence-based research is more important than ever, but it is not enough.

Because of the media environment and the nature of information in the twenty-first century, people are often able to produce some form of evidence to support whatever position they may take. This will only worsen in the near future with advances in artificial intelligence. The moment when "deep fake" videos are prevalent and increasingly hard to detect is not far off. What does this mean for the knowledge producers that remain committed to objectivity?

Two principal demands come to mind: First, there is a need for think tanks to get more rigorous and precise about what constitutes solid, evidence-based research. This will entail a recommitment to strict methodology. Universities and think tanks must double down on this endeavor. To be effective, research-based think tanks will have to get better at competing against the purveyors of fake news and alternative facts. Second, think tanks must improve how they communicate results. Famously, a 2014 World Bank study discovered that 31 percent of Bank reports had never been downloaded—not even once (Doemeland and Trevino 2014). If think tank policy recommendations are to have an impact, they have to be read.

"We tell ourselves stories in order to live," wrote Joan Didion. If think tanks are going to live and thrive in the fragmented and competitive information marketplace of the twenty-first century, they will have to tell better stories. They will have to articulate why their work is important and why now.

Finally, no attempt to peer into the future would be complete without recognizing the most consequential transformation happening today: the climate crisis. Think tanks of all kinds will have to account for the effects of climate change on their objects of study and the public policies they seek to shape. If the worst predictions come to pass, those effects will be pervasive in the century to come. Already, connections between climate change and the spread and impact of the COVID-19 pandemic are apparent. Wildlife habitat loss has been identified as a factor in its origins, and reduced air quality has contributed to an increased risk of complications for COVID-19 patients (Banerjee 2020). Over time, the effects of climate change will transform state priorities and social relations, and only the think tanks that prove up to the task of adjusting to this new reality will remain relevant.

The future is always uncertain, and change is inevitable. In the future, policymakers will be grappling with rapid political, technological, economic, and environmental change. As these trends continue to transform state and society—affecting how, by whom, and for what purpose we are governed—policymakers will require innovative thinking to navigate what will be largely uncharted terrain. In such a context, the need for independent, public-spirited thought leadership will be critically important. The risks are high, but the opportunities are many. The best think tanks are well-positioned to provide that thought leadership, but they must start preparing now. Their future will be determined by how well they do so.

References

Banerjee, Neela. 20 March 2020. Covid-19, Climate Change and Public Health: A Q & A with Aaron Bernstein. The Global Observatory. https://theglobalobservatory.org/2020/03/covid-19-public-health-climate-change-qa-with-aaron-bernstein/#more-20191.

Doemeland, Doerte, and James Trevino. 2014. Which World Bank Reports Are Widely Read? (English). Policy Research working paper; no. WPS 6851. Washington, DC: World Bank Group. http://documents.worldbank.org/curated/en/387501468322733597/Which-World-Bank-reports-are-widely-read.

Dorfman, Aaron, and Ellen Dorsey. 19 March 2020. Now Is the Time for Philanthropy to Give More, Not Less. The Chronicle of Philanthropy.

Kelstrup, Jesper Dahl. 2016. *The Politics of Think Tanks in Europe*. London: Routledge.

McIntyre, Lee. 2018. *Post-Truth*. Cambridge, MA: The MIT Press.

Milanovic, Branko. January/February 2020. The Clash of Capitalisms: The Real Fight for the Global Economy's Future. *Foreign Affairs*.

The Crisis of Liberalism and the Future of Think Tanks

Daniel Rothschild

Abstract Daniel Rothschild, Executive Director of the Mercatus Center at George Mason University in Arlington, VA, explores the Future of Think Tanks and Policy Advice in the United States.

Keywords Policy advice · Political actors · Think tanks

The future of think tanks in the United States is imperiled by dual crises of liberalism and of elite institutions. These crises present a fundamental challenge to think tanks as researchers, curators, guardians, and expositors of public policy ideas. Either a significant decline in normative liberalism or the continued faltering of elite institutions will render think tanks effectively unable to operate.

So far, think tanks have not sufficiently risen to the challenge.

D. Rothschild (✉)
The Mercatus Center at George Mason University, Arlington, VA, USA

J. McGann, *The Future of Think Tanks and Policy Advice in the United States*, https://doi.org/10.1007/978-3-030-60386-1_20

Threats to the Liberal Order
and a Crisis of Institutions

The liberal order in which think tanks, particularly in North America and Western Europe, came of age is under threat. The facts here are myriad and need not be recited extensively, but from the rise of illiberal right-wing and left-wing parties and factions (as well as some like Italy's Five Star Movement that defies traditional characterization) to a growing skepticism of what Jonathan Rauch calls liberal science, it's undeniable that the institutions, norms, and shared beliefs undergirding the liberal order are under threat (Rauch 1993).

This crisis of liberalism coexists with and mutually reinforces a crisis of institutions. Americans increasingly see institutions of all stripes as serving their own needs rather than those of the greater society. At best, this is a fundamental challenge to the utility of many public and private institutions. At worst, it represents a wholesale dismissal of many of those institutions as playing any legitimate role in public life.

Look for instance at trust in the leadership of institutions. According to data from the Pew Research Center, over 60 percent of Americans believe the following individuals act unethically some or most of the time: Members of Congress, journalists, leaders of technology companies, religious leaders, police officers, and local elected officials (Pew Research Center 2019). Additionally, more than 50 percent say that Members of Congress, local officials, tech company leaders, and journalists seldom if ever admit and take responsibility for mistakes (Pew Research Center 2019).

Gallup data suggest this decline in faith in institutional leadership spreads to institutions themselves. Taking 1995 as a baseline, confidence in newspapers has fallen from 30 to 23 percent, television news from 33 to 18 percent, the medical system from 48 to 36 percent, banks from 43 to 30 percent, and organized religion from 57 to 36 percent (Gallup 2019).

To my knowledge we don't have similar data on think tanks, but as a proxy we can look at higher education: confidence in colleges and universities has fallen from 57 to 48 percent just between 2015 and 2018 (Jones 2018). A majority of Americans in both parties as well as independents believe higher education is heading in the wrong direction (Parker 2019). University favorability ratings are underwater among both Democrats and Republicans.

The challenges to liberalism and to elite institutions are existential challenges to think tanks.

Think tanks are among the purest instantiations of liberal institutions, relying as they do on the liberal precepts of reason, evidence, persuasion, and argumentation. Further, think tanks by and large consist of, speak to, and are funded by elites.

Think tanks cannot meaningfully exist in an illiberal society, as their intellectual openness is by its very nature an affront to illiberal orders. (Witness the Chinese government's forcible closure of the market liberal Unirule Institute in 2019; it's a testament to the power of think tanks that a totalitarian state commanding an army of over 2 million saw a handful of economists, legal scholars, and analysts as an existential threat.) The American Enterprise Institute's motto, "A competition of ideas is fundamental to a free society," is one all think tanks could embrace.

Addressing These Critical Threats

What then should think tanks do to address these existential challenges? Let me make two suggestions.

The first is to exhibit greater epistemic humility. Many of our fellow citizens believe that the first two decades of the twenty-first century rebut the claims of experts to have knowledge that should be privileged over "common sense." In order to regain legitimacy among the public, think tanks should be more humble in the claims we make and avoid the temptation to push our conclusions too far.

Put simply: the public doesn't trust us, and we've given them ample reasons not to. We don't have all the answers, and we should not pretend we do.

Concomitantly, we should more clearly recognize that there are subjective decisions that fall beyond the boundaries of expertise. For instance, it seems likely that Brexit will reduce the United Kingdom's gross domestic product over the medium term, perhaps significantly—but experts can offer no opinion as to whether leaving the European Union was an objectively "correct" decision. Substituting expert judgement for democratic decision-making is deleterious to the public legitimacy of think tanks.

Think tank scholars should take a page from the work that earned Elinor Ostrom a Nobel Prize in economics: look for what's working in practice and seek to learn what from this can be generalized and applied elsewhere. Legal scholar Lee Anne Fennell coined

"Ostrom's Law": "A resource arrangement that works in practice can work in theory" (Fennell 2011). Look to the masses not just for problems, but for solutions: this was the animating spirit that guided my Mercatus Center colleagues who spent years documenting how bottom-up leadership was responding to rebuilding challenges after Hurricane Katrina (Boettke et al. 2007).

Secondly, think tanks can take an increasingly prominent role not just in offering policy advice but in articulating bold, positive, and actionable visions for our societies—and engaging in constructive debates with one another about the relative merits of these visions. This is an area that's increasingly neglected by the agenda setting institutions (particularly political parties) within many western democracies. Parties are increasingly willing to offer visions that meet perhaps one or two of these criteria, but few parties articulate visions that achieve all three simultaneously, and what passes for debate between them is long in ad hominem and scurrilous attacks and short on substance.

(It may seem that epistemic humility and vision setting are in conflict, but this isn't the case; the former involve positive claims, and the latter normative ideas. It's imperative to keep delineated these functions, which have always been played by think tanks to varying degrees. My argument is, in essence, that think tanks can simultaneously make more nuanced positive claims and bolder normative claims—carefully clarifying which claims are which.)

Why would think tanks take on this role? What makes think tanks particularly suited to developing and debating broader visions?

First, think tank analysts tend to consider reality a binding constraint; political actors and parties increasingly treat trade-offs, opportunity cost, state capacity, incentives, and democratic preferences (and even Constitutional text) as limitations that can be willed or wished away.

Second, in a time of increasing hyper-specialization, think tanks maintain an admirable degree of heterogeneity in terms of disciplines, experiences, values, and beliefs. While many think tanks have a general philosophical outlook, there exists significant and robust disagreement within most think tanks. (Indeed, this is a distinction lost by the press and the public, who are quick to apply pithy ideological labels to think tanks, vastly underestimating how much disagreement exists within.) Relative to most academic or political institutions, think tanks are more likely to bring together people with practical experience, academic expertise, political sensibilities, and communication skills. These traits—disciplinary hetero-geneity, spirited debate, and experiential diversity—make think tanks ideal for big picture intellectual foment.

Third, it may be critical for think tanks to regain some of the legitimacy that they, along with other elite institutions, have lost in the preceding years. Encouraging robust and productive debate between think tanks about policy priorities, visions of a good society, and our countries' and regions' places in the world can help think tanks be seen as participating in and strengthening democratic processes rather than trying to circumvent them.

A vision-setting role for think tanks is hardly revolutionary. The Heritage Foundation and the Center for American Progress arguably played greater roles in developing visions for the Republican and Demo-cratic Parties respectively over the last decades than the parties themselves (Levin 2012). London's Institute for Economic Affairs toiled for two decades to flesh out the political philosophy that came to be known as Thatcherism for the Prime Minister who embraced it (Levin 2012). My Mercatus Center colleagues Salim Furth and Emily Hamilton codirect a project developing a new vision of what American cities can be (Mercatus Center). While think tanks are typically associated with policy details, they in fact already do much vision development. Now is a perfect time to redouble these efforts.

THE LANDSCAPE GOING FORWARD

There remains a crucial role for think tanks in liberal democracies—but it's imperative that we change and adapt to the world around us. Two decades ago, think tanks could credibly claim to possess unique expertise; today, worldwide networks of experts and gifted laymen credibly chal-lenge this. A decade ago, political actors' plans generally had to at least pass a "smell test" that they could feasibly be enacted; not so today. And even five years ago, the liberal order seemed relatively secure; today it faces challenges not seen in a generation.

We must be clear about the challenge. There will be no reversion to the status-quo ante in another year, or after another election. This is not a matter of simply becoming better at social media, doing more promo-tional videos, or having snappier websites. The societies and communities in which think tanks live and work are undergoing a fundamental transformation. Think tanks can either aid that transformation or be swept away by it.

References

Boettke, Peter, Emily Chamlee-Wright, Peter Gordon, Sanford Ikeda, Peter Leeson, and Russell Sobel. 2007. The Political, Economic, and Social Aspects of Katrina. *Southern Economic Journal*. 74: 363–376.

Fennell, Lee Anne. 2011. Ostrom's Law: Property Rights in the Commons. *International Journal of the Commons* 5 (1): 9–27. http://doi.org/10.18352/ijc.252.

Gallup. 2019. Confidence in Institutions. Gallup. https://news.gallup.com/poll/1597/confidence-institutions.aspx.

Jones, Jeffrey M. 9 October 2018. Confidence in Higher Education Down Since 2015. Gallup. https://news.gallup.com/opinion/gallup/242441/confidence-higher-education-down-2015.aspx.

Levin, Yuval. 2012. "Devaluing the Think Tank." National Affairs.

Parker, Kim. 19 August 2019. The Growing Partisan Divide in Views of Higher Education. Pew Research Center. https://www.pewsocialtrends.org/essay/the-growing-partisan-divide-in-views-of-higher-education/.

Pew Research Center. 19 September 2019. Why Americans Don't Fully Trust Many Who Hold Positions of Power and Responsibility. Pew Research Center. https://www.people-press.org/2019/09/19/why-americans-dont-fully-trust-many-who-hold-positions-of-power-and-responsibility/.

Rauch, Jonathan. 1993. *Kindly Inquisitors: The New Attacks on Free Thought*. Chicago: University of Chicago Press.

The Future of Think Tanks: Trends and Transformations

James Manyika

Abstract James Manyika, Chairman of the McKinsey Global Institute in San Francisco, CA explores the Future of Think Tanks and Policy Advice in the United States.

Keywords Policy advice · Think tanks

The McKinsey Global Institute is about to mark its 30th anniversary. In taking stock of those three decades, I'm struck by how sharply the economic, societal, and technological context in which we operate has changed, especially in the years since the Great Recession. Every organization has been responding to disruptive change, and we are no exception. We have evolved in the topics we tackle, the way we work, how we communicate our findings, and our organizational structure.

For many years, analyzing productivity in different industries and national economies was MGI's bread and butter. But, as the world has gotten more complex, so have the research questions that we explore.

The global financial crisis of 2008, for example, underscored the world's interconnections and how they can produce value—but also

J. Manyika (✉)
McKinsey Global Institute, San Francisco, CA, USA

J. McGann, *The Future of Think Tanks and Policy Advice in the United States*, https://doi.org/10.1007/978-3-030-60386-1_21

transmit risk. Since then, we have regularly revisited the topic of global flows, illuminating trends in cross-country flows of finance, goods, services, data, and people. We also began tracking public, corporate, and personal debt by country. The recovery years have brought inequality and inclusiveness to the forefront, spurring us to look at economic mobility and the state of the social contract in multiple countries. As I write this, the COVID-19 pandemic has brought much of the global economy to a halt, challenging everyone in the world of think tanks to make sense of an unprecedented and fast-moving situation in real time. Think tanks can play an important role in bringing data and analysis to bear as we seek to address immediate needs, consider how to restart economies, and make sense of the "next normal."

With the global economic center of gravity shifting to China and an emerging Asia, the world is now multipolar. At MGI, we produce a steady stream of research specifically focused on China, India, and Southeast Asia. As major shifts change the structure of economies worldwide, we have examined topics such as what propels some developing nations toward faster growth, the role of manufacturing, labor's declining share of income, and the gig economy, as well as the impact of "superstar" companies, sectors, and cities. In each case, we find it important to not just examine macro trends but also to bring our unique micro-level perspectives on the interplay of individual firm decisions with those broader forces.

Perhaps no single factor has changed our world more dramatically than technology. We strive to help business and policy leaders prepare for what is over the horizon and to understand the broader economic and social implications of various technology trends. In recent years, we have produced major research reports on social media, big data, the Internet of Things, advanced analytics, advanced connectivity, and a multifaceted series on artificial intelligence. The research we've done on automation and the future of work, over multiple studies, has clearly resonated. It's been some of the most widely read and discussed work we've ever done, and it's helped some major organizations and governments start to think about the skills of the future and how to develop them. We assessed the factors affecting business decisions to adopt automation technologies, and in our midpoint scenario, found that some 400 million people worldwide could be displaced by automation over the next decade—and roughly 75 million may need to switch occupational categories and learn new skills.

More recently we have started exploring the potential for work to be performed remotely

In addition to documenting the changes shaping the world, MGI has had to respond to them in our daily work. We have broadened our footprint by adding more MGI partners, research teams, communications professionals, and council members in new parts of the globe (particularly Asia).

We're continually working out our own model of virtual, agile collaboration. Our teams are often scattered across multiple time zones, so it's not always easy to overlap, and we don't get to work together face-to-face as often as we'd like. But we try to turn this into a strength by passing the work from one person who's signing off to another whose day is just starting, with conference calls and virtual meetings during the overlap periods.

Tech overload is also contributing to shortening attention spans. Long, comprehensive reports remain our bread and butter; many of our regular readers still like to go deep. But like all think tanks, we have to reach out in other ways. The reports we published 15 years ago look almost quaint now. We have added infographics, photography, and more sophisticated visuals. We now produce a steady stream of short videos, data visualizations, multimedia presentations, and shorter-form, digital-first content. We had to develop our social media chops (and get used to the rough-and-tumble of open commentary), but now we have a robust presence on multiple platforms.

All of this has required us to add new types of talent and capabilities. Quantitative findings and business insights don't mean much if they don't get through to your audience. In a world of information overload, compelling writing and innovative design have never been more important in order to break through the noise. There's much more we can do to showcase our content digitally, and there is now a multitude of both traditional outlets and new digital channels where we can share our messages. MGI has been steadily adding more editorial, design, digital, and media professionals. They do much more than simply publish and disseminate our research. They work hand-in-hand with our research teams to develop the insights and make the end product reflect both the right brain and the left brain. To remain relevant and shape the public dialogue, think tanks have to continuously raise the bar for writing, design, and digital innovation.

The world of think tanks used to be relatively staid. But today we have a much more noisy, crowded marketplace of ideas with the proliferation of political think tanks, advocacy groups, and industry associations. On top of that, every large global company wants to be seen as a "thought leader," and to that end, many of them put out a steady stream of research and content—with some even setting up their own think tanks. The competition is a good thing, since it pushes all of us to up our game. It can also be valuable to see multiple complementary perspectives on complex topics, with insights developing much faster. With that being said, we try to stick to areas in which we believe we can add distinctive value. It may be tempting for think tanks to put out a perspective on every current event, but there is a real risk to diluting our traditional strengths by doing so.

We like to think that MGI occupies a special niche. We exist in that interesting space between business research and academic research, and we draw from both worlds. We are enormously fortunate in our access to data and quantitative tools. We also have the ability to move faster than academia—and that's often a must, given how many competing voices are out there in the same spaces we occupy. At the same time, our friends in business appreciate how deep we are still able to go.

McKinsey gives us a remarkable degree of latitude in the topics we choose to research, and because of its backing, we are free from the need to take commissioned work, solicit from donors, or compete for government grants. We recognize that this makes us extremely fortunate among think tanks, most of which have to devote significant time and resources to securing ongoing funding. We try to use that advantage wisely, addressing questions that matter to the global economy and to society as a whole. For example, we have explored how businesses are likely to automate work activities—and also pathways for retraining and redeploying displaced workers. In addition to the business uses of AI, we have considered how to address the biases it might perpetuate and how to harness it for social good, including breakthroughs in health care and biotechnology.

We call our method "micro to macro." As an arm of McKinsey & Company, we are uniquely positioned to tap into the expertise of colleagues who are observing the microeconomics on the ground as it's happening in real time. That micro-understanding of how business works allows us to have a better vantage point on macro trends. We grounded our recent research on trade and globalization, for instance, in a detailed examination of current trends in 23 industry value chains—and we will keep returning to this topic to explore how supply chains continue to evolve in a world in which resilience has suddenly become critically important. Every time we do a research project, academic advisors (including Nobel Laureates) critique, challenge, advise, and collaborate with us, helping us hold our work to the highest standards. There can be a great deal of value for any think tank in mixing and matching best practices from the private sector and academia.

Unlike organizations with a clear agenda, MGI is not focused on advancing a specific set of policies. We see our role as developing a fact base to inform leaders as they make policy and business decisions. Instead of offering policy prescriptions, we use our research findings to highlight the biggest issues they will need to solve and the tradeoffs they might have to make. Our partners spend much of their time traveling around the world to present our findings at conferences and have deep conversations with CEOs and government leaders—most of whom appreciate the chance to step back and look at the big picture.

Occasionally we are asked if it's discouraging to try to highlight facts at a time when the truth is malleable and audiences dismiss uncomfortable realities by labeling them as "fake news." But, in many ways, MGI feels energized. All of us feel keenly that the world is getting more complex, things are moving faster, and there are a lot of important problems to solve—from climate change to gender parity. The COVID-19 pandemic has driven home just how important it is to be agile and keep evolving as events dictate. We strive to take a fact-based, neutral, and rigorous approach. Today, that may be the most valuable contribution that we, or any think tank, can make.

Technology and Think Tanks: Survived the First Wave; Might not Survive the Second

Paul Salem

Abstract Paul Salem, President of the Middle East Institute in New York, NY, explores the Future of Think Tanks and Policy Advice in the United States.

Keywords Disinformation campaigns · Policy advice · Think tanks · Transparency

New technologies, social media, and profound changes in the informational and political landscape have posed serious challenges to think tanks.

How can think tank voices be heard in a world where every phone-carrier is a broadcaster? What is the leverage of evidence-based think tank research in a post-truth environment where neither fact nor logical argument is given the right of way?

How can think tanks influence a political environment deeply split into rival ideological and informational tribes and where positions are staked

P. Salem (✉)
Middle East Institute, Washington, D.C, USA

J. McGann, *The Future of Think Tanks and Policy Advice
in the United States*, https://doi.org/10.1007/978-3-030-60386-1_22

out regardless of the evidence or the argument? And how can think tanks survive in an environment where law firms, public relations firms, advocacy groups, spontaneous Facebook and Twitter communities, as well as foreign governments are all flooding the public sphere with their own policy positions and perspectives, or with misinformation spread by an army of bots?

However, despite all this, think tanks *have* survived; indeed in many cases, thrived. In the United States, the vast majority of think tanks in the foreign policy space—between Washington DC, New York, and other major cities of the United States—have survived the first two decades of this latest technological revolution, and the first three years of the political upending of 2016. And as the Go-To Global Think Tank Index shows, the number of think tanks continues to grow in the United States, and perhaps even more interestingly, around the world. The idea of the modern think tank—born in the US and the UK—is indeed a century old, but it still seems to have a present and a future in the first quarter of the twenty-first century.

Why might this be the case? How have successful think tanks adapted? And will there be other challenges in the next decades that think tanks might not be able to surmount?

To start with the last question first, the real turning point for think tanks will be when artificial intelligence and machine learning, drawing on big data, will be able to supplant human intelligence in examining vast areas of policy and suggest the best, most strategic and most detailed policy pathways forward. AI, algorithms and machines have already taken over high-speed decision-making in financial and stock markets, and have made their way into parts of military hyperwar decision-making. They are moving into medicine, law, various forms of research, and other fields previously thought to be the preserve of human intelligence. For example, it is not far fetched, or very long, before we see AI integrate and examine a sea of data in the foreign policy environment and come up with overwhelmingly researched and "argued" policy recommendations for confronting Russia, negotiating with China, or working through the various challenges of the Middle East.

And since AI and machine learning, as well as big data, require massive resources and will be a form of intelligence that is centrally owned and controlled—in China, by the state; in the United States, by the state and the Googles and Facebooks of the marketplace—think tanks will largely be left on the outside. From the vantage point of today, it is impossible to tell how, or if, think tanks can survive that future technological and civilizational shift.

In the meantime, a number of points are salient.

First, although technology has already had a massive impact on the information space, the marketplace and the political environment, policymaking is still made in the fairly traditional nineteenth and twentieth centuries way: persons elected or selected to office considering various priorities and pressures, weighing different policy options, and making a policy choice. What successful think tanks do is put themselves in the shoes—or minds—of the policymaker, exploit their own luxury of time and freedom from overwhelming pressures and deadlines, and think through various policy pathways.

This type of mental—and yes, we now must say it, *human* mental—work is still valuable to the harried policymaker. The policymaker certainly has her or his own set of perspectives, priorities, and political goals, and hence will very much pick and choose between the policy flavors on offer, but the policymaker also has a built-in need for pre-chewed—i.e., already examined and elaborated—policy choices.

Of course, most policymakers can draw from in-house policy kitchens, either in their government or in their political faction or party, from which to make their menu choices—and indeed some think tanks are in effect wholly part of political parties or factions. Independent think tanks are still valuable and useful in that they are like the delivery service of the policy world: as policymakers are in continuous need of policy options for fast changing policy challenges, the marketplace for production and consumption of policy proposals remains considerably larger than what in-house policy kitchens can monopolize.

Second, think tanks must learn, adopt, and integrate new technologies into their work; and indeed, many have done so. The recent wave of technological change has had a democratic aspect to it, in that it has made access to information, computing power, and communication accessible to anyone in the world with a smartphone, laptop, and an internet connection.

Think tanks have been both the victims and beneficiaries of this wave.

As victims, they are no longer the privileged institutions with access to enough information and communication platforms to make them easily stand out. They now must compete with an innumerable army of institutions, groups, and individuals who also have immediate access to all open source information in the world and have, in their cell phones or laptops, the tools to broadcast their own facts, opinions, analysis, and policy recommendations.

As beneficiaries, think tanks have also gained ready access to all open information around the world, and gained the capacity to communicate broadly and cheaply—through the written word, podcasts, videos, and social media—to audiences anywhere around their country or the world. And indeed, successful think tanks today have managed to integrate technology on the "input end" by leveraging technology in gathering and analyzing data; and on the "output end" by using technology to intensify and broaden the communication of policy views and recommendations. Of course, robust think tanks have also integrated technology into the internal management, transparency, and efficiency of their organizations.

As we have warned above, while the recent wave of technological change has had a democratizing and decentralizing aspect—in that it opened up access to information, computing power, and communication capacities previously the preserve of states or very large institutions—the oncoming AI revolution appears to have the reverse aspect, in that the massive computing engines necessary for AI will be available only to states and very large organizations.

Third, the "post fact" phenomenon which so greatly subverts the very idea of an evidence-based think tank bears some closer scrutiny. In an important way, it in itself is a "hoax"; in the sense that those who have created and been behind this phenomenon know quite well what they are doing: they are endeavoring to subvert the public's belief in certain facts or scientific realities for quite real and well-defined ends. The tobacco industry undermined the science that linked smoking to cancer not because it did not believe the science, but because it ran against its bottom line. Similarly, the Russian government pushes its disinformation campaigns to achieve well-defined objectives of undermining democracy as a model and the West as an alliance; and oil companies or low-tax extremists undermine climate change science to preserve well-defined interests of high profits and low-tax burdens. Such campaigns against truth are not new nor mysterious. The fact that the new information technologies have made the obfuscation of fact achievable in new ways is certainly a challenge, but does not necessarily indicate a fundamental change in the role of power and money in determining what the public believes to be true.

Finally, in the United States, we are passing through a particularly challenging moment, which is the Trump presidency. The challenge is not really in the "administration" per se, which might be ideological but also engages with policy debates and think tanks—at least from its own ideological corner—but in a president who seems, more than any other president before him, seriously detached from facts and logical argumentation, and even detached from his own policy kitchens and advisors. What is the point, many DC think tanks ask themselves in this era, of going through all the trouble of undertaking policy research, carefully considering policy pathways, and even successfully communicating and maybe convincing high government officials of those policy options, if, at the end of the day, the president will make major policy decisions on the spur of a call with a foreign leader or a Fox news segment.

None of us have seen this kind of presidency before. And it stymies the best efforts of ingenious think tankers. But in the longer term, it is also true that President Trump is unique, and that whatever new president takes office in 2021 or 2025 is likely to be closer to the norm.

In summation, think tanks certainly had to adapt nimbly to recent technological and political transformations; and they have been buffeted by the political transformations and peculiarities of the last few years, but most have adapted and survived, and many have thrived. They are likely to remain relevant in the next decade, and perhaps a decade or two beyond that. How they will fare—indeed will they survive in a recognizable form?—when the AI revolution fully moves into the policy realm, is the longer term question that looms over all think tanks, as it looms over schools, universities, media organizations, and most institutions of post-industrial civilization.

Increasing Relevance, Diminishing Access Require Unchanging Values for a Changing Audience

Adam Posen

Abstract Adam Posen, President of the Peterson Institute for International Economics in Washington, DC, explores the Future of Think Tanks and Policy Advice in the United States.

Keywords NGOs · Policy advice · Think tanks

Like many long-standing institutions in the United States, think tanks face unusual challenges in coping with an environment that did not exist even a decade ago. The collapse of faith in experts and expertise, as well as the increasing distrust of insiders, pose one set of problems. But, the Peterson Institute for International Economics and its sister institutions also face dramatic changes in the way that public officials in authority communicate to the public.

A. Posen (✉)
Peterson Institute for International Economics, Washington, DC, USA

J. McGann, *The Future of Think Tanks and Policy Advice in the United States*, https://doi.org/10.1007/978-3-030-60386-1_23

A necessary process of rethinking our role and the way we communicate is especially urgent for think tanks with headquarters in capitals–Washington, DC, in particular. It is in the nation's capital that think tanks have long relied on interaction with officials, ex-officials, and politicians to influence policy decisions. That was also part of how we got our ideas out to the public. We also became admittedly comfortable after many years of having our fortunes tied to a sort of golden era of the liberal consensus and a relatively open-minded US and European government structure. Leaders of think tanks and their backers have all meant well, but they never did question enough what had worked as an insider's game.

Now that authoritative voices are not as dominant as they once were, getting your voice out is difficult. So is getting funding. I think many of our colleagues in this collection of essays will recognize that there is a new demand for metrics and deliverables from funders, including individual philanthropists and new and old foundations. The successful funding of malaria nets by the Gates Foundation set a standard for measurable outcomes and direct impact that many donors now seek. They are less interested in funding applied research than they used to be. And to the degree that donors are interested in funding research on policy, they increasingly tend to seek it in-house, in their foundations and affiliates, or at universities that have moved into the policy space.

The Peterson Institute is determined to face these difficulties while living up to our mission. We wish to serve this mission of strengthening prosperity and human welfare in the global economy through expert analysis and practical policy solutions, as an independent nonprofit, nonpartisan research organization. So how have we gone about meeting these challenges?

When I was appointed president of the Peterson Institute in the summer of 2012, I had made clear to our board of directors that we had to adjust our direction and focus beyond Washington and even Western capitals. We had to make our content more accessible and change the kind of issues we were looking at. I consciously moved us substantively more into issues of inequality, human welfare, and political economy, for example. Of course, it goes without saying that we cannot compromise our quality or our objectivity in reaching these objectives, but we can change when the times demand that we change.

This obviously becomes the biggest issue in the communications sphere. First, reaching out to other parts of the world instead of focusing solely on Washington has great advantages. In some ways, it makes us more attractive as an employer because it gives our fellows a bigger audience and more and richer intellectual stimulus. Broadening the areas of research, I think, is exciting for people in the economics profession. But it has been a necessary adjustment.

As for our communications strategy, we have been fortunate to have support from the Peterson Foundation and other backers to make many changes. For example, Peterson Institute used to rely on what we would call the traditional book model to disseminate our scholarship. Every senior fellow used to have a book project or two on something like a two- to three-year cycle, and their books were reviewed in a few prominent publications. The authors would be in charge of promoting their books with speeches to select audiences and other forms of outreach. In these cases, the authors were responsible for producing anything more accessible to wider audiences derived from their work.

Like other think tanks, we have changed that model by increasingly bringing in communications experts, data visualization specialists, and editors to work with scholars in producing accessible products and offshoots, including blogs, infographics, explainers, social media content, and audiovisual versions of their work for broader outreach. We have done this while paying constant attention to the integrity of our scholarship, and we have achieved a good balance between traditional and nontraditional forms of communication.

Another area of recent innovation is in providing materials for educational institutions. PIIE had long thought about expanding in this area, but it was always decided that it was not to our comparative advantage or the most impactful thing in terms of influencing policy debates. But we are now committed to engaging at this broader level as well. We do not want to wag the dog by producing trendy materials on the world economy to maximize clicks. But we have committed in the last couple of years to new efforts to develop curriculum and self-education materials for the general public, in particular for higher education students.

We are also working to address the challenge of listening to voices beyond white Western capitals. From the time I started in this game in 1997, I have felt very privileged in the old sense. My native language is English, my degree is from a brand name US university, I have contacts from my policy experience, and therefore I have been invited to all kinds of places to hold forth. But think tanks and more importantly governments and NGOs outside the rich world are now rightly trying to promote their own countries' voices.

It is part of a rightful rebalancing of the share of voice and of advisory opportunities. For example, if you look closely at the TTCSP surveys, there is a healthy profusion of think tanks throughout the world. Of course, the selling propositions of some of them include providing access and currying favor. The think tank market is not perfect. But this broadening reflects a positive trend, and we can play a role by participating in these changes. Just as there are universities around the world and NGOs around the world, there should be think tanks around the world. I would also hope that the Peterson Institute for International Economics over time becomes increasingly considered not just an American think tank with global interests but a global public good.

To be frank, the current US Administration, as well as some other governments in the world, are making that objective easier for us even though they make our policy objectives harder to achieve in other ways. Throughout Democratic and Republican administrations in the Peterson Institute's nearly four decades of existence, we never played favorites, we never pandered, and yet we generally got a hearing in the highest US officialdom. I hope we never took that for granted, and we certainly never felt entitled to that status. We always knew we had to earn it. But until this Administration, we were always seen as being a part of the Washington establishment, and with that came a desire by top officials to engage with us.

Today, however, to the degree that we were viewed around the world as a way into the US government, some may see us as having gone down in value. But this also means that our standing up for the policy issues we care about in a consistent way, in an objective way, and in a transparent way, I believe, earns us more credibility around the world. And to some degree, standing up gets us better access in other governments, particularly international organizations like the European Commission, the International Monetary Fund, the World Bank, and the World Trade Organization. That access comes even when some of our work is about reforming them (unlike, at times, agencies run by elected officials).

In the final analysis, I do take some satisfaction that, even though I did not know how fast things were going to change, we in many ways did anticipate these shifts and were in favor of adapting to change. I have recruited both research and other professional staff with that in mind. The competition for talent and funding is extremely tough right now. But we have very strong backers, and our core backers are secure. In addition, because of our special focus on international economics, we are nearly unique among think tanks in our neighborhood. Other institutions cover a whole range of topics. That is their strategic choice. Our choice is to have a staff of senior fellows who broadly can understand what each other is doing and have a dialogue about it. Given our substantive focus, we also have a brand and a role that are very clear. That makes our identity and my job easier—and also, frankly, more fun.

This status still gives us the latitude to do some rethinking about both macroeconomic and trade policies, to broaden our perspectives, and to be more realistic, both in human and practical terms. This is a time when economics has become increasingly technical and mathematized. The field of economics increasingly requires not just specialized knowledge but specialized technique. I have long believed that the academic parts of the research profession have tended to reward creativity and cleverness and technique over relevance and robustness of work, which I believe are more important for public policy. And from the day I got here—well before I was president—I have tried to attract people to this institution who are at least open to that view.

So, consistent with our mandate, we view economics as a field of study connected to the issues of human welfare and material well-being. We have always been a home for economically literate political scientists and political economy experts of different stripes, and practitioners have been as much a part of our mix as distinguished economic academics.

Overall, the nationalism and skepticism we face today mean that think tank economists must approach the challenges I have outlined here with a bit of humility. We are trying to catch a moment when policy can move. We are trying to catch influential people's ears as well as those of the public. In the end, we have the honor of trying every day to advance ideas and policies that will prove beneficial for the people of the United States and the world.

Truth Decay: A Threat to Democracy and Think Tanks Alike

Michael D. Rich

Abstract Michael D. Rich, President and Chief Executive Officer of the RAND Corporation in Santa Monica, CA, explores the Future of Think Tanks and Policy Advice in the United States.

Keywords Policy advice · Public engagement · Research institutions · Think tanks

We are facing a crisis of trust in America. The number of people who say they have little or no confidence in Congress, the media, the Supreme Court, even public schools, is at or near historic highs. Asked to describe their feelings toward the federal government, a majority say either "frustrated" or "angry."

What is happening? The answer, I think, will shape the future of RAND, of think tanks in general, and most significantly, of the United States and the world. I have been calling it "Truth Decay." It's the declining role of facts and analysis in American public life, and it cuts much deeper than any political party or demographic. How are we going

M. D. Rich (✉)
RAND Corporation, Santa Monica, CA, USA

J. McGann, *The Future of Think Tanks and Policy Advice in the United States,* https://doi.org/10.1007/978-3-030-60386-1_24

to address climate change, defend our national security, and prepare for the next pandemic, if we can't even agree on basic facts?

I've always said that RAND is an idea as much as a research institute—a belief that the best way to solve the most complex and difficult problems is to begin with rigorous and objective analysis. In RAND's early days, that meant figuring out how to put a satellite into orbit, or how to manage the threat of global nuclear war. Today, it means saving lives from opioid misuse or gun violence, anticipating the challenges of new technology, and responding to the ever-changing risks of an ever-accelerating world. Our goal throughout has been to make communities around the world safer and more secure, healthier and more prosperous.

RAND was founded in the immediate aftermath of World War II, when few of what we now know as think tanks existed. Today, there are more than 1800 in America alone, many of them openly partisan or committed to advocating for or against some ideology or cause. If you need a report from a think tank to score a political or ideological point, there's a good chance you can find it.

The same thing has happened with the news media. The proliferation of cable news shows and social media sites has resulted in an echo chamber of voices that agree with us—or a shouting gallery of those that don't. The switch from one-hour network news programs to 24-hour coverage did not come with a 24-fold increase in reported facts.

In 2019, researchers at RAND asked hundreds of people around the United States where they get their news. The results were not encouraging. More than a quarter said they know where to go for reliable facts and information—sources like newspapers, for example, or television news shows. They just didn't have the time or the interest to bother.

That kind of disengagement has helped drive a wedge between what is true and what we think is true. Violent crime has been dropping for years in American cities, for example, but you would hardly be alone if you thought it has never been more dangerous to walk down the street. The scientific evidence for childhood vaccines has never been so strong, yet the World Health Organization recently listed vaccine hesitancy as one of the biggest threats to global health.

That's what I mean when I talk about Truth Decay. We have reached a point where our national discourse too often devolves into opinions about opinions, shouted across a cable-television split screen. We shouldn't be surprised that people use words like "frustrated" or "angry" to describe the national mood.

To be clear, this is not a problem for society as a whole; this is a problem that is especially prevalent in public policy. No business would make an investment without tuning out the noise and carefully reviewing every last cost and benefit. No baseball team would bring up a new second baseman without gathering every available data point. And yet, when it comes to the most important public policy issues we face, we let ourselves get distracted by ideology and emotion.

Take gun policy, for example. RAND decided a few years ago to review all of the evidence for and against some of the most common ideas for reducing gun violence—tougher background checks, for example, or weapon bans. We found that there was often a lack of reliable evidence either way. Federal constraints on gun research had created a factual vacuum around one of our most vociferous debates. Everyone was just shouting into the void.

But here's why I'm optimistic. That study caught the attention of the Laura and John Arnold Foundation (now called Arnold Ventures), which brought together a research consortium to invest up to $50 million in gun violence research. And Congress, which had resisted funding research into gun violence for 20 years, passed a bipartisan spending bill to provide $25 million more.

We've seen periods before in American history when the truth struggled to be heard. Some of those eras ended with new forms of journalism, recommitted to chasing down the truth and holding those in power to account. Others ended with government reforms aimed at winning back the trust of the governed. None of them ended without renewed faith in facts and analysis to guide public policy.

Research institutions like RAND are as important today as they ever have been. In part, that's because the problems we face demand a workforce of people who can collect and analyze data, think through the solutions, and provide recommendations without spin or bias. But it's also because, in fulfilling that role, think tanks can help restore facts and analysis to the center of American public policy.

The standards we set at RAND, for example—research that is transparent and clear, based on the best information, and temperate in tone—are meant to ensure that the bluest of blue-state Democrats and the reddest of red-state Republicans can trust our findings equally. We've made our research publicly available and free for decades so that anyone interested in climate change, gun violence, North Korea, or hundreds of other topics can access our facts and analysis for free.

We've also launched a major initiative to better understand the causes and consequences of Truth Decay—and most importantly, to devise solutions. We've looked at how the media has changed, how public engagement is evolving, why trust in institutions has fallen so far. We're approaching this like many of the other difficult policy problems that we confront every day—with facts and analysis.

The stakes could not be higher. As an old friend, a former chairman of the board at RAND, told me, RAND was established to deal with the existential threat of the time: the Soviet Union and its nuclear arsenal. Truth Decay, he said, is the existential threat of our time.

That, I believe, is the truth.

The Role of the Think Tank in Creating a More Equitable and Resilient Shared Future

Sarah Rosen Wartell

Abstract Sarah Rosen Wartell, President of the Urban Institute in Washington, DC, explores the Future of Think Tanks and Policy Advice in the United States.

Keywords Fundraising · Inclusive growth · Ivory tower · Policy advice · Policy analysis · Think tanks · Transparency

When President Lyndon B. Johnson founded the Urban Institute in 1968, he told the inaugural board, "Your job is to worry about the future" (Califano, Jr. 1991: 286). Little did he know just how much worrying the future would entail. Like us, our founders grappled with racism, inequality, war, and social upheaval. However, I doubt even they could have anticipated the ways in which a pandemic would lay bare the injustices that continue to threaten lives and futures in America today.

For decades, fact-based insights from think tank experts have guided how nations respond to and recover from crises. The essential think tank in the decades ahead will continue to focus on that, but also, and even more importantly, on how to make society more resilient to the disruptive

S. R. Wartell (✉)
The Urban Institute, Washington, DC, USA

© The Author(s) 2021   161
J. McGann, *The Future of Think Tanks and Policy Advice in the United States*, https://doi.org/10.1007/978-3-030-60386-1_25

threats of the future. The COVID-19 pandemic reminded us that our future is shared. We will recover and thrive when economic security and mobility, along with dignity and autonomy, are also shared.

Johnson commissioned the Urban Institute, in part, to assess whether his Great Society programs were working. He hoped that rigorous and independently conducted research would show that his agenda of anti-poverty solutions for people and communities was worthy of continued investment. Or, to put it as bluntly as Johnson did, he hoped that the evidence and new ideas would inspire American taxpayers to "ante up" for the poor long after he was gone.

Urban's mission remains the same today: to bring truth to bear and connect knowledge to action as we seek to improve lives and communities. The modern-day work of Urban's 500+ experts and social scientists is shaping practice in communities around the country and elevating the national debate. We are working alongside changemakers and bringing the power of evidence to find solutions to new challenges—even as our external environment changes with increased velocity.

Still, I worry. Is the Urban Institute ready for the world emerging around us? Are our sister institutions?

The Urban Institute and other think tanks have been building new tools and capacities for this changing world since long before we had heard of COVID-19. I believe we are ready to be put to the test.

Reaching the Ever-Expanding Audience of a Modern "Think Tank"

The old-fashioned moniker "think tank" now includes organizations playing myriad roles, as Jim McGann describes in *The Fifth Estate*—among them are policy analysis, new idea generation, ideological agenda setting, and empirical research, as Urban does principally (McGann 2016). We have different missions, purposes, business models, and points of view, but we share a common interest in making a difference.

These organizations have always sought relevance by informing decision-makers. But, not so long ago, power in America was closely held by a select few, and to shape policy and practice, one had to influence a relatively small number of actors. Key gatekeepers were found in elite media, academia, and the halls of power in Washington, and influencing them was an important but predictable art, accomplished through highly cultivated relationships, good media coverage, and publication in scholarly journals. Think tanks referred to this work as "dissemination," an inherently one-way information flow from a single source to a targeted audience.

In today's media and policymaking environment, information flows from many more places and in all directions—with social media delivering immediate feedback. What's more, too many of us receive information only from like-minded sources, making it far more challenging to reach and persuade those not already inclined to agree. With lower barriers to entry and more noise, it is challenging for think tanks to target all their relevant audiences and break through.

Recognizing the Emergence of New Change Agents

Today, power is more diffuse and less predictable than it was fifty—or even five—years ago. As we are seeing in the COVID-19 crisis, there are some things that only federal policy can tackle. But the critical importance of strong state and local leadership has been underscored as well. For over a decade, policy innovation has been driven from far outside the Beltway, by state legislatures and city mayors, a newly activated electorate, influential activists and celebrities, and even CEOs and corporate philanthropy. People in rural, non-coastal regions feel increasingly disconnected from wealthy coastal cities—and vice versa. Local leaders in each area are eager to set their own policy agenda. Social change is coming from all corners of society. Think tanks must have these broader, increasingly empowered audiences in mind when crafting their theories of change.

At Urban, we have benefited from expanding our reach and rolling up our sleeves alongside these new changemakers, asking what it would take to catalyze the bold solutions they seek. By convening leaders across different sectors and perspectives at the start of an inquiry, we bring new dimensions to our research questions. We must be crystal clear that we will follow the evidence where it leads; but by engaging at the front end, we increase the likelihood that research findings, when complete, will help guide new policies, practices, and investments. It is even more important that we do this in times of crisis, ensuring that we are answering the right questions and targeting solutions exactly where needed.

Understanding What It Means to Be Inclusive

A think tank's modern imperative requires that it do more than just reach people "in power." We must also understand who *does not* hold power, and why—and what roles organizations like ours play in either perpetuating or ending inequities.

Earlier this year, my colleagues Cameron Okeke and Nancy La Vigne pointed out: "Urban was established as an impartial, nonpartisan, and evidence-based voice for understanding and addressing pressing societal issues. But this noble mission was not developed in partnership with people living in marginalized communities" (Okeke and La Vigne 2019).

At Urban, we are slowly reckoning with what it means to be truly inclusive. Like most think tanks, we have a long way to go before our workforce—especially our senior leadership—reflects fully the changing face of America, and further yet to go to create a culture in which everyone feels like they belong and can be their full selves.

Being inclusive also requires that we do not just report what is happening in communities of color, but that we provide context on how racist policies over the decades continue to shape people's lives today and, without action, will continue to do so in the future (Urban Institute). When we fail to provide context, we may collectively perpetuate negative stereotypes. At Urban, we are examining our language for deficit mind-sets and developing communications guides to aid researchers when they write about justice involving LGTBQ, Black, LatinX, and other groups. And we are supporting researchers to take the time to examine the social structures that produce the conditions they find.

We are striving to put an equity lens on more and more of the research we conduct. As we analyze a candidate's proposal to forgive student loans, for example, we break down the implications by demographics, comparing which communities benefit most and least—and asking which proposal goes furthest in closing equity gaps.

Finally, inclusion does not just mean sharing our work with diverse communities; it means profoundly rethinking *how* we work. We must see lived experience as a valuable source of evidence. We are piloting new methods for community-engaged research. That means we are not just "studying" communities. We are turning to people within those communities as partners in the research process. We are working together to design research inquiries, collect data, interpret findings, and share insights and perspectives. When it comes time to share our findings, we don't paraphrase their experiences or put them in our own words. Rather, their experience is shared in *their* words and voices—at events, on panel discussions, in features, and in the reports themselves.

We must apply this equity lens, too, to the way we treat each other inside our organizations. This is a constant struggle: many of us experience discomfort in acknowledging personal power and privilege, recognizing implicit bias, and opening up to criticism and change. But change we must. As a community of scholars, there is tremendous potential for us all to use our authority to achieve equity, racial justice, and upward mobility. But, as Bryan Stevenson teaches, the path forward requires that we get comfortable being uncomfortable.

Understanding the Risks and Possibilities of New Technology

Many think tanks are tackling the social and policy implications of technology: privacy, cybersecurity, geopolitical relationships, artificial intelligence (AI), and much more. Moving our work, education, and much of the economy almost entirely online for months has laid bare vast inequities in technology access and fluency. And we increasingly see how technology could further institutionalize inequality. For example, evidence shows that some algorithms used in hiring software can perpetuate the racial inequities a candidate has faced in the past. Biased software has also been known to lead policymakers to unfairly target some neighborhoods instead of others. Flawed inputs lead to flawed conclusions. By combining a growing understanding of the mechanisms of structural racism with access to new data sources and an understanding of the mechanisms of new technology tools, we can scrutinize how these capacities are deployed and ultimately inform changemakers about how to do so responsibly.

At the same time, we must search for ways to deploy technology as a tool to expand opportunity. For example, we know that algorithms can help employers quickly find those with relevant competencies without using the proxy of privileged credentials. Rapidly testing and responsibly evaluating tech tools for good is an emerging role for data-driven think tanks like Urban.

Harnessing Technology and Data for Better Evidence and Research

Technology also offers new pathways for researchers and think tank experts to gather insight and accomplish their work. Businesses and the academy are using big data and AI to study virtually everything, yet think tanks are only just beginning to embrace cutting-edge technological tools and computational science in analysis. But the pandemic has also taught us that these tools can help—for example, to gather real-time information for decision-makers when every day counts.

At Urban, we are not only exploiting new data sources for immediate policy insight but also using vast processing power to accelerate the pace of insight from existing tools. For years, we have built powerful microsimulation models that answer what-if questions about who benefits when state and federal policymakers make changes to our health and economic safety net. Cloud computing makes our forecasting tools more powerful, allowing us to run many thousands of policy scenarios at once and thereby greatly expanding our understanding of policy choices. And we can create externally facing tools that allow any user to explore the tradeoffs of policy choices, just as we do. For example, our researchers at the Urban-Brookings Tax Policy Center turned their microsimulation model into an accessible tool for exploring the Tax Cuts and Jobs Act (TCJA). Users can explore hypothetical adjustments to the TCJA to better understand how policy variation would have affected—and could affect in the future—the after-tax incomes of different kinds of families.

Sharing our privileged access to information with the public is a moral imperative for the modern think tank. Responsible "think tank" leadership in data science lies in democratizing access to information. At Urban, we have built portals for huge datasets that allow everyone to pull and compare data quickly—eliminating the weeks of expert work it once took simply to make fields compatible. Urban's Education Data Explorer draws from multiple datasets—Common Core of Data, Civil Rights Data Collection, and College Scorecard, among others—and allows users to personalize this information by school, district, or college. The purpose of this portal, and others, is to make it easier for researchers, practitioners, and policymakers to generate accurate insights from a trusted source.

Responsible think tanks also must obtain the technological sophistication to protect privacy when maintaining and mining big data. Transparency (with privacy) can build confidence too. By visualizing data in engaging ways, our audiences directly interact with the content and deepen their own understanding of who wins and who loses under different outcomes. And, we hope, greater transparency and deeper engagement with the evidence could help build renewed trust in the facts that are the bedrock of our society.

PROTECTING INDEPENDENCE FIERCELY

To do all of the above, think tanks—regardless of business model—need resources. Most nonprofit leaders know well the pressure of fundraising, which requires that we find alignment with donor interests. But if we are not careful, that quest for resources can divert us from the mission, and, at the extremes, risk our organizations' hard-won credibility. Think tanks must fiercely guard their independence at all times. At Urban, we hold fast to published funding principles and carefully explain to funders, over and over, that, while we gladly listen to all perspectives, our experts' conclusions and findings are theirs *alone*. Think tank leaders must protect expert independence, even—and *especially*—when the conclusions are unexpected or unwelcome to some in power.

PAIRING FACTS WITH FEELINGS RESPONSIBLY

There is no doubt in my mind that facts matter now more than ever. Popular assertions to the contrary, there remain steadfast audiences for evidence-based decision-making. The events of 2020 starkly illustrate that we ignore facts at our peril. Facts help us understand complex problems and craft solutions to seemingly intractable challenges. They help us predict how potential policy change could transform lives for better or worse. And they hold us all accountable if solutions fall short.

But we know that facts are not enough to drive change. Today's scholars do not belong in an ivory tower, and research does not belong on a shelf or a website.

It is not enough for us to generate evidence and assume that audiences will find and act on it. We need more than facts to build trust and understanding. We must ground our research and ideas in the reality of life around the country and in the challenges faced by families and their communities. We must embrace both scientific and ethnographic methods, using stories to uncover relationships that we can test through rigorous data analysis. Then, we must explain what facts and evidence mean through interactive, multimedia, easy-to-digest reports, tools, and features—and through stories that help audiences relate through shared human experience. And, we must cede our own privilege and bring other voices forward as well as our own.

Once Again, Thinking About the Future

Even before the COVID-19 pandemic, powerful shifts in technology, demographics, climate, and the global economy threatened to exacerbate and harden inequalities and block opportunities to thrive. Unease about these disruptions has fueled a level of polarization not seen for a century and derailed progress on racial and economic injustices that have been too long at the center of the American story.

Post-pandemic, our attention will be turned by necessity to recovery from great health and economic crises. But I worry about what will happen if we, as leaders, thinkers, and doers in the think tank community, fail to seize the moment and harness these disruptive forces of change, not simply to rebuild, but also to strengthen society and make it more resilient to disruption in the future. Think tanks have a critical role to play in illuminating our interdependence and the strength we gain from equity and inclusion. And our scholars and experts can examine, quickly discard, or further develop the most promising solutions to the issue that weighs heavy on hearts and minds today: What would it take to create a more resilient and equitable future? How can we leverage technology and demographic change for inclusive growth and shared prosperity? Can we put forces of change to work for our values? It is incumbent upon all of us to help redesign a future in which everyone can realize their potential to contribute, feel valued, and have a voice.

REFERENCES

SUBMISSIONS

Califano, Joseph A. 1991. *The Triumph and Tragedy of Lyndon Johnson*. New York: Simon & Schuster Inc.

Okeke, Cameron, and Nancy G. La Vigne. 8 April 2019. Reckoning with Structural Racism in Research: LBJ's Legacy and Urban's Next 50. Urban Institute. https://www.urban.org/urban-wire/reckoning-structural-racism-research-lbjs-legacy-and-urbans-next-50.

CONCLUSION

McGann, James G. 9 February 2016. 2015 Global Go to Think Tank Index Report. Scholarly Commons, University of Pennsylvania. Accessed November 7, 2018. https://repository.upenn.edu/think_tanks/10/.

The World—And the Workplace—Are Changing: Our Mission Stays the Same

Jane Harman

Abstract Jane Harman, Director, President, and CEO of the Wilson Center in Washington, DC, explores the Future of Think Tanks and Policy Advice in the United States.

Keywords Policy advice · Think tanks

This year the future came early. I never imagined the Wilson Center would become a virtual workplace on my watch. The COVID-19 pandemic has tested governments, hospitals, businesses, workers, and families around the world, and it has forced think tanks to move online until further notice.

It has also forced us to reconsider what think tanks are all about. On the surface, the Wilson Center is a place to gather experts, policy-makers, and the public for in-person meetings. But at the core, our role is to inform and educate. That's something we can do from anywhere thanks to modern technology. Ironically, this crisis has brought us and

J. Harman (✉)
The Wilson Center, Washington, DC, USA

© The Author(s) 2021
J. McGann, *The Future of Think Tanks and Policy Advice in the United States*, https://doi.org/10.1007/978-3-030-60386-1_26

our audiences closer, and our programs are seeing it as an opportunity for innovation.

Governments across the world may be disenchanted with globalization. But for the Wilson Center and its peers, it's more important than ever to integrate—not silo—our regional experts. Coronavirus is just the latest reminder that unexpected global crises have become the new normal. Until we invent a crystal ball to see the future, our best chance at predicting the next crisis involves getting our regional experts to work together on a cross-cutting basis.

To that end, the Wilson Center's strategic plan spurs our regional programs to work together across four issue areas at the top of policymakers' dockets: digital threats and opportunities, great power competition, rule of law, and Arctic cooperation.

This month, the pandemic has quickly become the fifth issue. The crisis has been an unforeseen but opportune moment to try out our cross-cutting lens. Our Ground Truth Briefing (GTB) series, which is a telephonic discussion of breaking news with scholars on the ground in various regions, lends itself well to social distancing guidelines. Many of our programs have already reenvisioned their in-person events as GTBs. And rather than covering the usual niche issues in, say, Latin America or Russia, our events offer a comprehensive picture of how each region around the world is responding to the virus.

The Wilson Center engine can stay running thanks to fast, widespread internet service and reliable mobile networks. But those networks are about to get a lot faster. In another example of our cross-cutting research, our Science and Technology Innovation Program, Mexico Institute, and Canada Institute are working together to explain the potential of next generation 5G networks and help lawmakers across North America make the most of data and technology sharing provisions in the new NAFTA, or USMCA.

Earlier this month, Canada became the third and final country to ratify the trade pact. But now comes the hard part: implementing the new rules. Our experts are advocating for the creation of a North American Technology Trust in the form of innovation hubs in each of the three countries; procedures for aggregating data generated in each country and using it to power machine learning systems; a legal framework for sharing tech ideas; and an annual summit to help the project along (King and

Rosen 2019). We're also producing infographics to spread the word about 5G fundamentals, supply chains, and geostrategic competition. Finally, our programs are planning a roundtable listening tour in each North American country over the next year to understand the policy implications of 5G and how we can work better together. As the tech landscape changes, we and our peers need to leverage our regional and issue-based expertise to capture the whole picture of tomorrow's possibilities.

Technology isn't the only landscape that's changing. The Arctic is also a center of greener—or icier—pastures. The Wilson Center's Polar Institute houses the Arctic Infrastructure Inventory, an exhaustive database of up to $1 trillion in infrastructure projects (think: roads, ports, energy facilities) that await investment. Alongside the Arctic Economic Council's Arctic Investment Protocol, the inventory helps guide investment and research into environmentally sustainable growth in the region and the emerging Arctic Ocean. That's where our other regional experts come in, explaining how countries like Russia and China are angling for influence in the new waterway. When navigating the Arctic, all hands are on deck.

From the unprecedented COVID-19 pandemic, to the promise of new technologies, to sustainable development of the Arctic and much more, our experts are keeping their ears to the ground and the public informed. The Coronavirus is far from the last crisis that the world will face. On top of that, globalization, emerging technologies, and political fragmentation will further challenge our traditional notions of what a think tank does. Think tanks of the future need to get creative about how they gather audiences, convene global policymakers, and generate cross-cutting solutions—and they need to do it fast.

Former Chicago Mayor Rahm Emanuel once famously said, "Don't let a crisis go to waste." The Wilson Center is not.

REFERENCE

SUBMISSION

King, Meg, and Jake Rosen. 16 July 2019. Building a North American Technology Trust. *Yale Journal of International Affairs*. http://yalejournal.org/article_post/building-a-north-american-technology-trust/.

Conclusions

Are Think Tanks Fit for an Uncertain Future?

James McGann

Abstract James McGann, Director of the Think Tanks and Civil Societies Program, Lauder Institute for Management and International Studies, University of Pennsylvania in Philadelphia, PA, explores the Future of Think Tanks and Policy Advice in the United States.

Keywords Civil society · Fundraising · Policy advice · Think tanks

Throughout the last six to eight years, the world witnessed a rise in populism, nationalism, and protectionism; all signaling a challenge to the post-WWII order and multilateralism. At the same time, transnational challenges—such as: growing trade tensions, economic turbulence, increasing economic inequality, climate change, mass migration, and

Electronic supplementary material The online version of this chapter (https://doi.org/10.1007/978-3-030-60386-1_27) contains supplementary material, which is available to authorized users.

J. McGann (✉)
Think Tanks and Civil Societies ProgramLauder Institute for Management and International Studies, University of Pennsylvania, Philadelphia, PA, USA

J. McGann, *The Future of Think Tanks and Policy Advice in the United States*, https://doi.org/10.1007/978-3-030-60386-1_27

refugee crises, as well as traditional and nontraditional security threats—demand that countries and institutions cooperate more frequently and effectively. In the past five months, we have been forced to deal with a pandemic that not only threatens our lives and livelihoods, but also demands that think tanks around the world respond.

We are entering a period of significant change, uncertainty, and instability, where the previously established order—as well as the international organizations that work to sustain relative peace and prosperity—are under assault. Meanwhile, enduring and emerging existential and transnational threats are growing. The post-WWII economic, political, and security order is being challenged and redefined by national and regional tectonic shifts in domestic and international politics. Presently, we are living through a dynamic moment in world history. As such, it is important to take stock of the technological, political, economic, and organizational trends and disruptions that are taking place in real time. The COVID-19 crisis and the economic, political challenges that follow will test think tanks like they have never been tested before. These unprecedented times provide us with an opportunity to assess the cross-sectional issues and trends in order to develop effective responses. These are daunting challenges, and so it is essential that we marshal our intellectual and institutional resources to prepare for the turbulence and turmoil that we are likely to face in the upcoming decade.

There are four key trends that flow from the 4th Industrial Revolution that will ultimately transform all of our jobs and lives over the next ten years. These four forces drive the digital and political disruptions that are sweeping across the globe. They are:

- The disruptive power of social media, artificial intelligence, and big data;
- The dramatic increase in the rate of technological change;
- The increased velocity of information and policy flows; and
- The promise and the peril of the Information Age and the 4th Industrial Revolution.

Human and digital networks, such as the Internet, are constantly enhanced by new technologies that increase both the volume and velocity of information flows around the world. In this world of rapid-moving information, it is possible to manage and manipulate massive amounts of data, to the effect of disrupting business, politics, and public policy. Henry Kissinger famously said that being a policymaker is like being at the end of a fire hose. Today, we are all at the end of a high pressure stream of information.

These trends in information and technology serve as a catalyst that fuels the political discontent and disruptions which are on the rise in the United States, France, Britain, Italy, the Philippines, Hungary, Brazil, and other countries around the world. Policymakers have erroneously attributed the source of this discontent as the backlash against global-ization. In reality, it is much more complex and it involves a number of issues and problems that—thanks to the internet, social media and social networks—have become omnipresent and inescapable. The increasing uncertainty of our time has created a sea of insecurity, making people concerned and confused about the future of their work and well-being. This sea of insecurity consists of seven factors that have intensified over the last seven to 10 years. The failure of government or elected officials to address these issues, due to political polarization and policy paralysis, has left citizens around the world disillusioned and discontent. These factors help explain why people are gravitating to nontraditional politi-cians who promise security and quick fixes to complex problems. The sea of insecurity is composed of the following factors:

1. **Economic Insecurity**: Jobs, entire careers, and professions are being reengineered—or simply vanishing. The income gap is growing and the opportunities for the current generation may not be as promising or secure as it was for us or our parents.
2. **Physical Insecurity**: We are reminded on a daily—even hourly—basis of terrorist attacks, the impact of climate change and other catastrophic events, such as the prospects of a nuclear conflict. This increases the collective sense of insecurity.
3. **Loss of National and Personal Identity**: Changing demographic patterns—namely, regular and irregular migration—are raising ques-tions about national identity. In twenty years, Asians, Hispanics and those of European descent will be of equal numbers in the United States. Similar changes are taking place in Europe. This change is disconcerting to many and is compounded by other economic and social factors.
4. **The New World Disorder**: The balance of power that was charac-teristic of the Cold War and bipolarity provided a degree of order

and security that is currently missing. History tells that the most unstable and dangerous periods are the ones in which there are multiple power poles or those in which powers are rising and falling. We are in precisely such a period: everyone is in charge—and no one is.

5. **Information Insecurity**: The Information Age has given us unprecedented access and convenience, but this comes at the cost of privacy, security, loss of identity, and—to a certain extent—humanity. The flood of information, which includes disinformation, misinformation, and attempts to manipulate portions of the population, makes us feel uncertain and insecure. Advancements in technology will also change the way we live and fight, but also the way our world is organized.

6. **Constant and Disruptive, Change**: We live in an age of unprecedented change and disruption, where technology has accelerated the rate of change and, essentially, made change the only constant in people's lives. In addition, the rise of new powers and a shift in the center of gravity of economic, military, legal, social and political influence, from the global North and the West further fuels insecurity. In brief, we are currently undergoing a fundamental reassessment of how power and influence is expressed through the world. These changes permeate every aspect of our lives and are profoundly unsettling, leaving many feeling adrift and insecure.

7. **The Insecurity of No Answers and No Escape**: The most unsettling aspect of all is the inadequacy of our leaders and institutions, neither of which are focused on these key issues. They are not addressing these concerns; it is therefore no mystery why there has been a loss of trust and confidence in governments and elected officials. This is where think tanks can play a critical role, by helping to create policy answers and action that is needed in many societies today. Think tanks play a critical role in analyzing, developing, and promoting policy solutions, particularly in times of extreme disruption and change. However, these organizations now operate in information-rich societies where facts, evidence and credible research are often ignored—and where disinformation is gaining influence.

Let me be clear: the future is not bleak, and I am convinced that emerging technologies will help solve many of the world's problems, whether they be pandemics, water and food shortages, or climate change. Think tanks need to be on the front lines, not the side lines, by helping to analyze these issues and prepare society for the transformative changes we face now and in the future. To remain relevant and impactful, think tanks and policy institutes must simultaneously pursue rigor, innovation, accessibility, and accountability more than ever before. In short, think tanks must adapt and innovate by transforming their organizations to be smarter, better, faster, and more mobile. We should always keep in mind that for each disruption, a window of opportunity opens to create new products, a larger audience, and new ways of implementing policy. Think Tanks should approach every challenge by asking: "What can we learn from this? What can I do differently? How can we turn adversity into an opportunity for growth and change? Think tanks can provide a range of strategies and best practices for transforming public policy and institutions, even in an era of digital and political disruptions, as well as increasing social and economic turbulence. While these challenging times, there is also an opportunity for those institutions that can develop new and innovative solutions to the complex problems we face.

New Business Models for Think Tanks

Think tanks today face increasingly intense political and technological changes in the world, all of which pose serious challenges and even existential crises. In 2015, a Washington Post columnist, Amanda Bennett, asked "are Think Tanks obsolete?" (Bennett 2015). To answer this question: think tanks are not obsolete, but some of their strategies are. In order to overcome the numerous predicaments imposed by the current era, think tanks must innovate their business models. The goal of this study is to highlight some of the critical threats and opportunities that think tanks face globally, by those who are grappling with them on a daily basis: the senior executives of some of the leading think tanks around the world. These threats are best expressed by the so-called "four mores": more issues, more actors, more competition, and more conflict. These indicate the challenges that all think tanks will face: competitive challenges, resource challenges, technological challenges, and policy challenges. Ultimately, effective responses to these threats and opportunities should focus on the "Five M's": mission, market, manpower, mobility, and money. In the global marketplace of ideas, think tanks need to develop national, regional, and global partnerships while also creating new and innovative platforms to deliver their products and services to an ever-expanding audience of citizens, policymakers, and businesses around the world. The think tanks that are innovative and agile will be the ones best positioned to seize the opportunities that this new and dynamic policy environment presents to think tanks across the globe.

A New Operational Context

Today, think tanks face the "NGO pushback" in which external forces are using legal and extralegal means to limit the number, role, and influence of civil society. This "pushback," coined in the 2015 Global Go To Think Tank Report, resulted, in part, from the rise of partisan politics and political polarization. These forces eroded effective decision-making and blurred the lines between policy advice and advocacy for think tanks (McGann 2015: 11). The general public, influenced by this partisanship and the rise of populism, has expressed a distrust in higher power institutions, including research institutes such as think tanks. The funding landscape for think tanks has also changed drastically. The so-called "golden age" of think tanks in the seventies and eighties is gone. Today, with the recent rise of global philanthropy, donors focus more on projects that are short term, specific, and high impact (McGann 2015: 11). Furthermore, in the face of rapid technological advancements, think tanks now find themselves no longer the only actor in the knowledge brokerage industry, but as the sole of its competitors in the "global marketplace of ideas," vying with other actors such as media organizations, advocacy groups, consulting and law firms (McGann 2015: 11). Given this context, adapting new business models seems inevitable and, therefore, worth studying. Frankly, the traditional academic-centric model has come to an end. The business models for think tanks is transitioning from "the manner by which the think tank delivers value to stakeholders, entices funders to pay for value, and converts those payments to research with the potential to influence policy" to a condign that incorporates innovative strategies in management, communication, financing, and technologies, all without undermining the quality and rigorousness of research and publication (Ralphs 2016).

Management

The leadership of think tanks is being called to change. The desire for a scholarly head of a think tank, like the motto previously maintained, "research it, write it, and they will find it," no longer holds true. Today, think tanks not only need scholars, but also managers. In a world of research, where the competition for ideas and influence is intense, think tanks need to demonstrate the value they add to public discourse and public policy. The competition that think tanks face today has led some funders to decide that they are only willing to fund the products and services of think tanks that have the "highest impact." In today's environment, everyone can be a think tank—at least virtually. Think tanks face competition from advocacy organizations, for-profit consulting groups, and law firms, in addition to every means of electronic competition—an increasingly efficient competitor (Ralphs 2016). As noted in the 2015 Global Index Report, "Big data, which involves the collection and analysis of massive amounts of information to pinpoint critical data and trends, may render think tanks and their staffs superfluous. This new analytic capability enabled by supercomputers, maybe the think tanks of the future" (McGann 2016: 15). However, big data, and any other competitors cannot replace the potential insight that only an organization devoted solely to policy research can generate. Accordingly, think tanks must figure out how to market their product most effectively.

Think tank executives hold vast influence over the direction their institution takes. In the wake of these global shifts, all of which directly impact think tanks, executives need to wield their influence with these challenges in mind.

Strategic Communication

There are at least three audiences with which think tanks must communicate—donors, policymakers, and the general public. In order to catch the attention of these key audiences, a think tank must be able to deliver the analytical information it promises in a timely and effective manner.

In an age of near-instant information dissemination via social media, think tanks must keep pace. Active blogging, social media use, online interactive forums, and infographics are examples of methods to achieve this. Once a think tank has garnered attention on social media platforms and more generally online, they simultaneously raise their donor profile. As funding becomes an issue, the burden falls heavily on the public image of the institution. Thus, strategic communication of the goods and services that a think tank can offer is an important way of maintaining necessary funding. These communication strategies are the vehicles in delivering research results, and as such, are crucial in generating an impact on the policymaking community (Kuntz 2013: 23).

INNOVATIVE FUNDING STRATEGIES

While Benjamin Franklin wrote: "...nothing can be said to be certain, except death and taxes," think tank leaders today may say "...nothing can be said to be certain, except death and short-term project funding"— if any funding is to be certain at all (Avins 2013). Increasingly, think tanks are moving toward endowment-based funding in order to increase long-term stability. Other executives have suggested the establishment of funds, such as a shared reserves fund or an emergency bridging fund, to help think tanks build capacity and avoid financial risks. In short, an effective and successful fundraising strategy should build the organizational strategy and related processes into researchers' everyday work: for example, having a Monitoring and Learning (M&L) system in place that communicates real impact while generating useful information and more importantly, be explicit about the connection between the strategy and funding needs.

BIG DATA ANALYTICS

Accompanying technological advancements is the increasing amount of data and the use of big data analytics. Some estimations suggest a 4300% increase in annual data generation by 2020—44 times greater in 2020 than it was in 2009 (Numanović 2017). According to studies conducted by the European Parliament Research Service in 2016, big data analytics could identify efficiencies that can be made in a wide range of sectors, leading to innovative new products, greater competitiveness, and economic growth (Numanović 2017: 3). The McKinsey Global Institute (MGI) stressed that "there are no industries in which the ability to continuously integrate new sources of data of any format and quality would not generate improvements" (Henke et al. 2016: 73). Think tanks are no exception.

While there are certainly complex regulatory concerns and technical loopholes with the appearance of new technologies, big data analytics could help think tanks better measure their influence in a quantitative way. In 2016, Tsinghua University in China released the 2016 Big Data Report on Chinese Think Tanks, which measured the influence of Chinese think tanks by assembling 110 thousand websites, 18 million active WeChat—a Chinese social media app—official accounts, 150 million active Weibo—the so-called "Chinese Facebook"—accounts, 6155 online forums, and 930 thousand news Apps for smartphones (Zhu 2017: 24). This effort suggests that the seemingly immeasurable "influence" of think tanks could be measured into a quantifiable number of citations, articles, and mentions on various platforms—a technique that, while limited, could be adopted and used to gain more insights regarding the communication strategies and level of social and political impact of think tanks.

CONCLUSION

In order to survive these ever-escalating changes, think tanks recognize the need for constant innovation more and more. With the understanding that the global context is constantly changing, think tanks should push to innovate management tactics, strategic communication plans, fundraising strategies, and big data analyses. On the other hand, this new business model should not go against think tanks' original mission to produce quality and influential research, intended to help policymaking. Think tanks need to find a delicate balance between innovating their business models and committing to the quality and rigorousness of their research and products. None of this should come at the expense of the other. It is only with an innovative business model and unwavering commitment to the excellence of research that think tanks will be able to survive and excel in today's world.

REFERENCES

INTRODUCTION AND LITERATURE REVIEW

McGann, James G. 2015. *Global Think Tank Innovations Summit Report: The Think Tank of the Future is here Today*. Philadelphia: Think Tanks and Civil Societies Program, University of Pennsylvania.

CONCLUSION

Avins, Jeremy. 25 November 2013. Strategy Is a Fundraising Necessity, Not a Luxury. *On Think Tanks*. Accessed 7 November 2018. https://onthinktanks.org/articles/strategy-is-afundraising-necessity-not-a-luxury/.

Bennett, Amanda. 5 October 2015. Are Think Tanks Obsolete? *The Washington Post*. Accessed 7 November 2018. https://www.washingtonpost.com/news/in-theory/wp/2015/10/05/are-think-tanksobsolete/?noredirect=on&utm_ter&utm_term=.20802394eb95.

Henke, Nicolaus, Jacques Bughin, Michael Chui, James Manyika, Tamim Saleh, Bill Wiseman, and Guru Sethupathy. December 2016. The Age of Analytics: Competing in a Data-driven World. McKinsey Global Institute. Accessed 6 November 2018. https://www.mckinsey.com/business-functions/mckinsey-analytics/our-insights/theage-of-analytics-competing-in-a-data-driven-world.

Kuntz, Fred. 11 July 2013.Communications and Impact Metrics for Think Tanks. Centre for International Governance Innovation. Accessed 7 November 2018. http://www.cigionline.org/articles/communications-and-impact-metrics-think-tanks.

McGann, James G. 9 February 2016. 2015 Global Go to Think Tank Index Report. Scholarly Commons, University of Pennsylvania. Accessed November 7, 2018. https://repository.upenn.edu/think_tanks/10/.

Numanović, Amar. 11 July 2017. Data Science: The Next Frontier for Data-Driven Policy Making? Medium. Accessed 7 November 2018. https://medium.com/@numanovicamar/https-medium-com-numanovicamar-datascience-the-next-frontier-for-data-driven-policy-making-8abe98159748.

Ralphs, Gerard. 14 June 2016. Think Tank Business Models: The Business of Academia and Politics. *On Think Tanks*. Accessed 7 November 2018. https://onthinktanks.org/articles/think-tank-business-models-the-business-ofacademia-and-politics/.

Zhu, Xufeng. 23 June 2017. A New Ranking: The 2016 Big Data Report on Chinese Think Tanks. *On Think Tanks*. Accessed 7 November 2018. https://onthinktanks.org/resources/a-new-ranking-the-2016-big-data-report-onchinese-think-tanks/.

Appendix

Author Biographies

AHMED Masood Masood Ahmed is president of the Center for Global Development. He joined the Center in January 2017, capping a 35-year career driving economic development policy initiatives relating to debt, aid effectiveness, trade, and global economic prospects at major international institutions including the IMF, World Bank, and DFID. Ahmed joined CGD from the IMF, where he served for eight years as director, Middle East and Central Asia Department, earning praise from Managing Director Christine Lagarde as a "visionary leader." In that role, he oversaw the Fund's operations in 32 countries, and managed relationships with key national and regional policymakers and stakeholders. In previous years, he also served as the IMF's director of External Relations, and deputy director of the Policy Development and Review Department. From 2003 to 2006, Ahmed served as director general, Policy and International at the UK government's Department for International Development (DFID). In that role, he was responsible for advising UK ministers on development issues and overseeing the UK's relationship with international development institutions such as the World Bank. Ahmed also worked at the World Bank from 1979 to 2000 in various managerial and economist positions, rising to become Vice President, Poverty Reduction and Economic Management. In that role he led the

J. McGann, *The Future of Think Tanks and Policy Advice in the United States*, https://doi.org/10.1007/978-3-030-60386-1

heavily indebted poor countries (HIPC) debt relief initiative, which has to-date brought relief from debt burdens to 36 of the world's poorest nations. Born and raised in Pakistan, Ahmed moved to London in 1971 to study at the LSE where he obtained a B.Sc. Honors as well as an M.Sc. Econ with distinction. He is a UK national. Ahmed is a leading expert on Middle East economics, having served on the Advisory Board of the LSE Middle East Center, as well as on the World Economic Forum's Global Agenda Council on the Middle East and North Africa. He has also participated in CGD's Advisory Board.

ALLEN John R. John R. Allen currently serves as the 8th president of the Brookings Institution. He is a retired U.S. Marine Corps four-star general and former commander of the NATO International Security Assistance Force and U.S. Forces in Afghanistan. Prior to his role at Brookings, Allen served as senior advisor to the secretary of defense on Middle East Security and as special presidential envoy to the Global Coalition to Counter ISIL. Allen is the first Marine to command a theater of war, as well as the first Marine to be named commandant of midshipmen for the U.S. Naval Academy.

Beyond his operational and diplomatic credentials, Allen has led professional military educational programs, including as director of the Marine Infantry Officer Program and commanding officer of the Marine Corps Basic School. Allen was the Marine Corps fellow to the Center for Strategic and International Studies and the first Marine officer to serve as a term member of the Council on Foreign Relations, where today he is a permanent member.

Among his other affiliations, Allen is a senior fellow at the Merrill Center of the Johns Hopkins School of Advanced International Studies and a senior fellow at the Johns Hopkins Applied Physics Laboratory. He is an "Ancien" of the NATO Defense College in Rome, and a frequent lecturer there. Allen is also the recipient of numerous US and foreign awards.

He holds a Bachelor of Science in operations analysis from the U.S. Naval Academy, a Master of Arts in national security studies from Georgetown University, a Master of Science in strategic intelligence from the Defense Intelligence College, and a Master of Science in national security strategy from the National Defense University.

ALLISON Graham Graham Allison is the Douglas Dillon Professor of Government at Harvard University where he has taught for five decades. Allison is a leading analyst of national security with special interests in nuclear weapons, Russia, China, and decision-making. Allison was the "Founding Dean" of Harvard's John F. Kennedy School of Government, and until 2017, served as Director of its Belfer Center for Science and International Affairs which is ranked the "#1 University Affiliated Think Tank" in the world. As Assistant Secretary of Defense in the first Clinton Administration, Dr. Allison received the Defense Department's highest civilian award, the Defense Medal for Distinguished Public Service, for "reshaping relations with Russia, Ukraine, Belarus, and Kazakhstan to reduce the former Soviet nuclear arsenal." This resulted in the safe return of more than 12,000 tactical nuclear weapons from the former Soviet republics and the complete elimination of more than 4000 strategic nuclear warheads previously targeted at the United States and left in Ukraine, Kazakhstan, and Belarus when the Soviet Union disappeared.

As "Founding Dean" of the modern Kennedy School, under his leadership, from 1977 to 1989, a small, undefined program grew 20-fold to become a major professional school of public policy and government.

As Assistant Secretary of Defense under President Clinton and Special Advisor to the Secretary of Defense under President Reagan, he has been a member of the Secretary of Defense's Advisory Board for every Secretary from Weinberger to Mattis. He has the sole distinction of having twice been awarded the Distinguished Public Service Medal, first by Secretary Cap Weinberger and second by Secretary Bill Perry. He has served on the Advisory Boards of the Secretary of State, Secretary of Defense, and the Director of the CIA.

Dr. Allison's latest book, *Destined for War: Can America and China Escape Thucydides's Trap?* (2017), is a national and international bestseller. His 2013 book, *Lee Kuan Yew: The Grand Master's Insights on China, the United States and the World*, has been a bestseller in the United States and abroad. *Nuclear Terrorism: The Ultimate Preventable Catastrophe*, now in its third printing, was selected by the *New York Times* as one of the "100 most notable books of 2004." Dr. Allison's first book, *Essence of Decision: Explaining the Cuban Missile Crisis* (1971), ranks among the all-time bestsellers with more than 500,000 copies in print.

BURNS William William J. Burns is president of the Carnegie Endowment for International Peace and the author of the national bestseller, *The Back Channel: A Memoir of American Diplomacy and the Case for its Renewal* (Random House, 2019). He retired from the U.S. Foreign Service in 2014 after a thirty-three-year diplomatic career, as only the second serving career diplomat in history to become deputy secretary of state. Prior to his tenure as deputy secretary, Ambassador Burns served from 2008 to 2011 as undersecretary for political affairs. He was ambassador to Russia from 2005 to 2008, assistant secretary of state for near eastern affairs from 2001 to 2005, and ambassador to Jordan from 1998 to 2001. Ambassador Burns earned a bachelor's degree in history from La Salle University and master's and doctoral degrees in international relations from Oxford University, where he studied as a Marshall Scholar. He and his wife, Lisa, have two daughters.

CARTER Ash Ash Carter is a former United States Secretary of Defense and the current Director of the Belfer Center for Science and International Affairs at Harvard Kennedy School, where he leads the Technology and Public Purpose project. He is also an Innovation Fellow and corporation member at MIT.

For over 35 years, Secretary Carter has leveraged his experience in national security, technology, and innovation to defend the United States and make a better world. He has done so under presidents of both political parties as well as in the private sector.

As Secretary of Defense from 2015 to 2017, he pushed the Pentagon to "think outside its five-sided box." He changed the trajectory of the military campaign to deliver ISIS a lasting defeat, designed and executed the strategic pivot to the Asia-Pacific, established a new playbook for the United States and NATO to confront Russia's aggression, and launched a national cyber strategy.

Secretary Carter spearheaded new technological capabilities and a more agile approach to the relationship between the Pentagon and the tech sector. He also transformed the way the Department of Defense recruits, trains, and retains quality people, opening all military positions to women without exception.

He earned a BA from Yale University and a Ph.D. in theoretical physics from Oxford University as a Rhodes Scholar.

DJEREJIAN Edward The Honorable Edward P. Djerejian's Foreign Service career spanned eight US administrations, from John F. Kennedy to William J. Clinton. Prior to his nomination as US ambassador to Israel, he was assistant secretary of state for Near Eastern affairs in both the George H.W. Bush and Bill Clinton administrations. He was previously the US ambassador to the Syrian Arab Republic. He also served as special assistant to President Ronald Reagan and as deputy press secretary for foreign affairs in the White House. Following his retirement from government service, Djerejian became the first director of Rice University's Baker Institute for Public Policy, where he is also the Janice and Robert McNair Chair in Public Policy. He is the author of "Danger and Opportunity: An American Ambassador's Journey Through the Middle East." He has been awarded the Presidential Distinguished Service Award; the Department of State's Distinguished Honor Award; the Ellis Island Medal of Honor; the Anti-Defamation League's Moral Statesman Award; the Award for Humanitarian Diplomacy from Netanya Academic College in Israel; the National Order of the Cedar, bestowed by President Émile Lahoud of Lebanon; the Order of Ouissam Alaouite, bestowed by King Mohammed VI of Morocco; and the Order of Honor, bestowed by President Serzh Sargsyan of Armenia. He is also a recipient of the Association of Rice Alumni's Gold Medal for his service to Rice University. Djerejian was a member of the board of trustees of the Carnegie Corporation of New York (2011–2019) and is a fellow of the American Academy of Arts and Sciences.

FEULNER Edwin J. Edwin J. Feulner, Ph.D., is the founder and former president of The Heritage Foundation. Feulner was a founding trustee of Heritage and served as its president from 1977 to 2013 and again for a brief period in 2017. Feulner's work in the conservative movement has earned him praise from world leaders, including President Ronald Reagan, who said of him, "He has helped to shape the policy of our government."

Feulner has served in a multitude of roles over the years, including as former president and treasurer of the Mont Pelerin Society, a trustee and former chairman of the board of Intercollegiate Studies Institute, a board member of the Institut d' Etudes Politiques, a life member of the board of trustees of Regis University in Denver, past president of the Philadelphia Society, and a member of the advisory board of the

Public Diplomacy Collaborative at Harvard University's Kennedy School of Government. He is also a longtime officer and director of the Sarah Scaife and Thomas A. Roe foundations. He was confirmed by the U.S. Senate on three separate occasions, first as chairman of the U.S. Advisory Commission on Public Diplomacy, then as vice chairman of the National Commission on Economic Growth and Tax Reform, and as a member of the Congressional Commission on International Institutions and the Gingrich-Mitchell Congressional U.N. Reform Task Force.

Feulner graduated from Regis University with a double major in English and business and received an MBA from the University of Pennsylvania's Wharton School of Business in 1964. He later attended Georgetown University and the London School of Economics and then earned his doctorate at the University of Edinburgh in 1981. Feulner is a frequent public speaker throughout the United States and abroad. He has received honorary degrees from 10 universities and has received honors from the governments of Taiwan, South Korea, and the Czech Republic. He has written nine books, the most recent of which is titled *The American Spirit*. He also was awarded the Presidential Citizens Medal from President Ronald Reagan in 1989.

FINLAY Brian Brian Finlay is the President and Chief Executive Officer of the Stimson Center. Under his tenure since 2016, Stimson has transformed its business model, launched pioneering new engagements across Asia, and industry-defining programming on environmental security, renewable energy, and technology. As a result, the Center has tripled in size and continues to dramatically outperform similarly sized institutions in global rankings. Notably, Stimson today boasts the most diverse and inclusive workforce of any major Washington think tank.

Brian previously served as Vice President, Managing Director, and Senior Fellow at Stimson. Prior to joining the Center, he served as executive director of a Washington-based lobbying initiative focused on counterterrorism issues, as a researcher at the Brookings Institution, and as a program officer at the Century Foundation. Prior to emigrating to the United States from his native Canada, Brian served with the Public Health Agency and the Department of Foreign Affairs and International Trade. He Chairs the Board of Directors of iMMAP, an information management and data analytics organization focused on improving humanitarian relief and development coordination. Brian was an adjunct professor at American University in Washington, and today sits on the Editorial Board of Global Security, a journal of health, science and policy published by Routledge, Taylor & Francis. With expertise in nonproliferation, transnational crime, counter-trafficking, and supply chain security, Brian holds an M.A. from the Norman Patterson School of International Affairs at Carleton University, a graduate diploma from the School of Advanced International Studies, the Johns Hopkins University and an honors B.A. from Western University in Canada.

HAMRE John John Hamre was elected president and CEO of CSIS in January 2000. Before joining CSIS, he served as the 26th US deputy secretary of defense. Prior to holding that post, he was the undersecretary of defense (comptroller) from 1993 to 1997. As comptroller, Dr. Hamre was the principal assistant to the secretary of defense for the preparation, presentation, and execution of the defense budget and management improvement programs. In 2007, Secretary of Defense Robert Gates appointed Dr. Hamre to serve as chairman of the Defense Policy Board, a post he served under four secretaries of defense.

Before serving in the Department of Defense, Dr. Hamre worked for 10 years as a professional staff member of the Senate Armed Services Committee. During that time, he was primarily responsible for the oversight and evaluation of procurement, research, and development programs, defense budget issues, and relations with the Senate Appropriations Committee. From 1978 to 1984, Dr. Hamre served in the Congressional Budget Office, where he became its deputy assistant director for national security and international affairs. In that position, he oversaw analysis and other support for committees in both the House of Representatives and the Senate. Dr. Hamre received his Ph.D., with distinction, in 1978 from the School of Advanced International Studies at Johns Hopkins University in Washington, DC, where his studies focused on international politics and economics and US foreign policy.

HARMAN Jane Jane Harman, the Director, President, and CEO of the Wilson Center, is an internationally recognized authority on US and global security issues, foreign relations and lawmaking. She resigned from Congress on February 28, 2011 to join the Woodrow Wilson Center as its first female Director, President, and CEO. Representing the aerospace center of California during nine terms in Congress, Harman served on all the major security committees: six years on Armed Services, eight years on Intelligence, and eight on Homeland Security. During her long public career, Harman has been recognized as a national expert at the nexus of security and public policy issues, and has received numerous awards for distinguished service.

She is a member of the Defense Policy Board and the Homeland Security Advisory Committee. She also serves on the Executive Committee of the Trilateral Commission and the Advisory Board of the Munich Security Conference.

Harman is a Trustee of the Aspen Institute and the University of Southern California. She is also a member of the Presidential Debates Commission.

A product of Los Angeles public schools, Harman is a magna cum laude graduate of Smith College, where she was elected to Phi Beta Kappa, and Harvard Law School. Prior to serving in Congress, she was Staff Director of the Senate Judiciary Subcommittee on Constitutional Rights, Deputy Cabinet Secretary to President Jimmy Carter, Special Counsel to the Department of Defense, and in private law practice.

She has four adult children and eight grandchildren.

HERRMANN Victoria Dr. Victoria Herrmann is the President and Managing Director of The Arctic Institute. In addition to managing the Institute and Board of Directors, her research and writing focus on climate change, community adaptation, resilient development, and migration. Victoria has testified before the U.S. Senate, served as the Alaska Review Editor for the Fourth National Climate Assessment, contributes to The Guardian and Scientific American on climate policy, and was named one of the most 100 influential people in climate policy worldwide in 2019 by Apolitical. She has published in many peer-review journals and her expert opinion has appeared on CNN, BBC, and NPR among others. Victoria currently serves as the Principle Investigator of the National Science Foundation funded Arctic Migration in Harmony: An Interdisciplinary Network on Littoral Species, Settlements, and Cultures on the Move, a major international initiative to integrate discipline-isolated research on changing Arctic migration patterns and advance knowledge on the movement of peoples, economies, cultures, and ecosystems catalyzed by environmental variability. Beyond the Arctic, Victoria studies climate-induced displacement, migration, and relocation in North America and Fiji as a National Geographic Explorer. In her first National Geographic project, America's Eroding Edges, she traveled across the country interviewing 350 local leaders to identify what's needed most to safeguard coastal communities against the unavoidable impacts of climate change. Her project, Rise Up to Rising Tides, is creating an online matchmaking platform that connects pro bono experts with climate-affected communities. The project seeks to safeguard heritage by connecting national expertise to some of the 13 million Americans at risk of being displaced due to rising waters in the coming years.

She serves on the Arctic Research Consortium of the United States' Board of Directors, on the Steering Committee of the Climigration Network, and as an IF/THEN Ambassador for the American Association for the Advancement of Science. As an Assistant Research Professor at Georgetown University's School of Foreign Service, Victoria teaches environmental communication; science communication at the University Centre of the Westfjords, Iceland; and public speaking at National Geographic Sciencetelling Bootcamps. She was previously a Junior Fellow at the Carnegie Endowment, a Fulbright Awardee to Canada, a Mirzayan Science and Technology Policy Fellow at the National Academies of Sciences, and a Gates Scholar at the University of Cambridge, where she received her Ph.D. in Geography.

JAMES Kay Coles Mrs. Kay Coles James has an extensive background in crafting public policy and leading in nearly every sector of America's economy. She has worked at the local, state, and federal levels of government in the administrations of former US President George H. W. Bush (1989–1993), former Virginia Governor George Allen (1994–1996), and former US President George W. Bush (2001–2005), and she has also served dozens of organizations in the corporate, and nonprofit arenas. Mrs. James was also appointed by President Donald J. Trump to serve on the National Women's Suffrage Commission.

Today, Mrs. James is the President of The Heritage Foundation, America's premier conservative think tank. The Heritage Foundation is dedicated to formulating and promoting conservative public policies based on the principles of free enterprise, limited government, individual freedom, traditional American values, and a strong national defense. Mrs. James has also been a trustee of The Heritage Foundation for 14 years.

Mrs. James is also the founder of The Gloucester Institute, an organization which trains and nurtures college-aged leaders in minority communities. She has served as a Senior Fellow and Director of The Citizenship Project at the Heritage Foundation, the Senior Vice President of the Family Research Council, and as the Executive Vice President and Chief Operating Officer for One to One Partnership.

A graduate of Hampton University, Mrs. James is the recipient of numerous honorary degrees, including a Doctor of Laws from Pepperdine University, the University of Virginia's Publius Award for Public Service, and the Spirit of Democracy Award for Public Policy Leadership from the National Coalition on Black Civic Participation. As a commentator and lecturer, Mrs. James has appeared on network morning shows and several national news and talk programs. She is the author of three books: her award-winning autobiography *Never Forget* (1993); *Transforming America from the Inside Out* (1995); and *What I Wish I'd Known Before I Got Married* (2001).

KEMPE Fredrick Frederick Kempe is the President and Chief Executive Officer of the Atlantic Council. Under his leadership since 2007, the Council has achieved historic, industry-leading growth in size and influence, expanding its work through regional centers spanning the globe and through centers focused on topics ranging from international security and energy to global trade and next generation mentorship.

Before joining the Council, Kempe was a prize-winning editor and reporter at the Wall Street Journal for more than twenty-five years. In New York, he served as assistant managing editor, International, and columnist. Prior to that, he was the longest-serving editor and associate publisher ever of the Wall Street Journal Europe, running the global Wall Street Journal's editorial operations in Europe and the Middle East.

In 2002, The European Voice, a leading publication following EU affairs, selected Kempe as one of the fifty most influential Europeans (although he is American), and as one of the four leading journalists in Europe. At the Wall Street Journal, he served as a roving correspondent based out of London; as a Vienna Bureau chief covering Eastern Europe and East-West Affairs; as chief diplomatic correspondent in Washington, DC; and as the paper's first Berlin Bureau chief following the unification of Germany and collapse of the Soviet Union.

As a reporter, he covered events including the rise of Solidarity in Poland and the growing Eastern European resistance to Soviet rule; the coming to power of Mikhail Gorbachev in Russia and his summit meetings with President Ronald Reagan; the wars in Afghanistan, Iraq, and Lebanon in the 1980s; and the American invasion of Panama. He also covered the unification of Germany and the collapse of Soviet Communism.

He is the author of four books. The most recent, Berlin 1961: Kennedy, Khrushchev, and the Most Dangerous Place on Earth, was a New York Times Best Seller and a National Bestseller. Published in 2011, it has subsequently been translated into thirteen different languages.

Kempe is a graduate of the University of Utah and has a master's degree from Columbia University's Graduate School of Journalism, where he was a member of the International Fellows program in the School of International Affairs. He won the Columbia Graduate School of Journalism's top alumni achievement award and the University of Utah's Distinguished Alumnus Award.

For his commitment to strengthening the transatlantic alliance, Kempe has been decorated by the Presidents of Poland and Germany and by King Carl XVI Gustaf of Sweden.

LAIPSON Ellen Ellen Laipson is the Director of the International Security program at the Schar School of Policy and Government at George Mason University. She joined GMU after a distinguished 25-year career in government and as President and CEO of the Stimson Center (2002–2015). She serves on a number of academic and other nongovernmental boards related to international security and diplomacy, and is a columnist for worldpoliticsreview.com. Her last post in government was Vice Chair of the National Intelligence Council (1997–2002). She also served on the State Department's policy planning staff, the National Security Council staff, and worked at the Congressional Research Service for more than a decade. A member of the Council on Foreign Relations, she serves on the Advisory Councils of the International Institute of Strategic Studies, the Chicago Council on Global Affairs, and Georgetown University's Institute for the Study of Diplomacy. She was a member of the CIA External Advisory Panel from 2006 to 2009, President Obama's Intelligence Advisory Board from 2009 to 2013, and on the Secretary of State's Foreign Affairs Policy Board 2011–2014. Laipson has an M.A. from the School of Advanced International Studies, Johns Hopkins University and an AB from Cornell University.

LUPEL Adam As Vice President and COO at IPI, Dr. Lupel is responsible for developing IPI's long-term research agenda and for overseeing management of the Programs, External Relations, Communications, and Finance teams and coordination among IPI's offices in New York, Vienna, and Manama in close collaboration with the President. Between 2014 and 2016 he served as the director of research and publications for the Independent Commission on Multilateralism.

Dr. Lupel also conducts research on issues related to globalization and the multilateral system. He is the author or co-editor of three books: *Globalization and Popular Sovereignty: Democracy's Transnational Dilemma*, *Peace Operations and Organized Crime: Enemies or Allies?*, and *Responding to Genocide: The Politics of International Action*.

He is a member of the Editorial Boards of *International Peacekeeping* and *Constellations: An International Journal of Critical and Democratic Theory*; Politics and Human Rights Advisory Board Member of Manhattan Marymount College; and Advisory Board member of The International Center for Multigenerational Legacies of Trauma.

Prior to 2006, when he joined IPI as Editor, he was the Managing Editor of *Constellations: An International Journal of Critical and Democratic Theory*, and he taught modern and contemporary political theory at The New School's Eugene Lang College in New York. He has a Ph.D. in political theory and an MA in liberal studies from the New School for Social Research and a BA in international relations with a concentration in Latin America from Boston University.

MANYIKA James James Manyika is a senior partner at McKinsey & Company, chairman of the McKinsey Global Institute (MGI), and a member of McKinsey's board of directors. Based in Silicon Valley for over 20 years, James has worked with the chief executives and founders of many of the world's leading technology companies on a variety of issues that include strategy and growth, business transformation, and innovation. At MGI, James has led research on technology, the digital economy, the future of work, as well as on productivity, competitiveness, and the global economy. Early in his career, James published a book on AI and robotics, recently another on global economic trends, and numerous articles and reports. He has served along with technologists, business leaders, economists, and policymakers around the world on several task forces and commissions related to technology and an inclusive economy.

James was appointed by President Barack Obama to serve as vice chair of the Global Development Council at the White House, and by US Commerce Secretaries to the Commerce Department's Digital Economy board of advisers and the National Innovation Advisory Board. He serves on the boards of the Council on Foreign Relations, the Broad Institute of MIT and Harvard, and is involved in other research activities and advisory boards at Stanford, Harvard, MIT, and Oxford. He is also involved in various philanthropic activities, including serving on the boards of the MacArthur Foundation, Hewlett Foundation, and Markle Foundations.

A Rhodes Scholar, James received his D.Phil., M.Sc., and M.A. from Oxford in AI and robotics, mathematics, and computer science, and his B.Sc. in electrical engineering from the University of Zimbabwe as an Anglo-American Scholar. He is a fellow of the American Academy of Arts and Sciences, a fellow of the Royal Society of Arts, a distinguished fellow of Stanford's AI Institute, and a fellow of DeepMind.

James is trustee of the Aspen Institute, a member of the Trilateral Commission, and has been a nonresident senior fellow of the Brookings Institution in Economic Studies. He was a visiting scientist at NASA Jet Propulsion Labs, and a faculty exchange fellow at MIT. At Oxford, he was a member of the Programming Research Group, the Robotics Research Lab, and elected a research fellow of Balliol College.

McGANN James James G. McGann is a Senior Lecturer of International Studies at the Lauder Institute, Director of the Think Tanks and Civil Societies Program and a Senior Fellow at the Fels Institute of Government at the University of Pennsylvania. Dr. McGann has served as a consultant and advisor to the World Bank; the United Nations; the Asian Development Bank; the United States Agency for International Development; the Soros, Rockefeller, MacArthur, Hewlett and Gates foundations; the Carnegie Corporation; and foreign governments on the role of nongovernmental, public policy and public engagement organizations in civil society. He has served as the Senior Vice President for the Executive Council on Foreign Diplomats, the Public Policy Program Officer for the Pew Charitable Trusts, the Assistant Director of the Institute of Politics, John F. Kennedy School of Government at Harvard University. He also served as a Senior Advisor to the Citizens' Network for Foreign Affairs and the Society for International Development. Dr. McGann earned his M.A. and Ph.D. from the University of Pennsylvania. He has authored over 15 books on think tanks and is the creator and editor of the annual Global Go To Think Tank Index.

POSEN Adam During Dr. Posen's presidency, the Peterson Institute has won global recognition as the leading independent think tank in international economics, including repeated top rankings from the Prospect Think Tank Awards and the Global Go To Think Tank Index. Under his leadership, PIIE has expanded to include 42 world-renowned resident and nonresident fellows and increased its endowment by 50 percent. Since 2013, PIIE has developed high-level recognition and research partnerships in the People's Republic of China, while deepening longstanding ties with policymakers in other East Asian, European, and North American capitals. The Institute also has broken new ground in providing accessible economic analysis to the general public.

RICH Michael D. Michael D. Rich is president and chief executive officer of the RAND Corporation, a nonprofit, nonpartisan research organization that helps improve policy and decision-making through research and analysis. For more than 40 years, Rich has helped RAND become a leading source of expertise, analysis, and evidence-based ideas in an increasingly complex and polarized policymaking environment.

Rich began his career at RAND as a summer intern in 1975, joining the organization full-time the following year as a researcher focused on US national security issues. He has served in a variety of senior leadership positions at RAND and was instrumental in the creation of the RAND National Defense Research Institute, a federally funded research and development center that provides research and analysis to the Office of the Secretary of Defense, the Joint Staff, the Unified Commands, the Navy, the Marine Corps, the defense agencies, and the Intelligence Community. He also helped lead RAND's diversification and expansion into international markets—including the establishment of RAND Europe, the RAND Qatar Policy Institute, and RAND Australia.

Since becoming president and CEO in 2011, Rich has focused on extending the impact of RAND's work—challenging the organization to broaden its legacy of innovation and helping decisionmakers stay ahead of the curve on the issues that matter most. A champion of RAND's commitment to help improve the quality of decisionmaking,

Rich co-authored a 2018 report titled *Truth Decay* that examines how the diminishing role of facts and analysis in American public life has caused an erosion of civil discourse and political paralysis, among other problems.

Throughout his career, Rich has also been an enthusiastic supporter of the Pardee RAND Graduate School, the world's largest Ph.D. program in policy analysis, where he teaches and advises graduate students and has chaired numerous committees.

Rich serves on the governing boards and advisory committees of many policy and service organizations, including the Council for Aid to Education, the International Institute for Strategic Studies, the Los Angeles World Affairs Council, WISE & Healthy Aging, the Everychild Foundation, Santa Monica–UCLA Medical Center and Orthopaedic Hospital, and the UCLA Foundation. He is also a member of the U.S. Defense Science Board, the Council on Foreign Relations, and the California Bar.

Rich received his B.A. from the University of California, Berkeley, and his J.D. from the University of California, Los Angeles.

ROTHSCHILD Daniel Daniel M. Rothschild is the Executive Director of the Mercatus Center at George Mason University. He leads strategy and oversees all programs and operations for the organization.

Mr. Rothschild was previously director of state projects and a senior fellow with the R Street Institute and director of external affairs and coalitions at the American Enterprise Institute. Previously, he spent six years in a variety of policy, communications, and project management positions at the Mercatus Center. He has worked extensively with think tanks throughout the country.

His popular writing and articles and reviews have appeared in the *Wall Street Journal, Reason, Weekly Standard, Roll Call, The Hill, Chicago Policy Review, Economic Affairs,* and many other popular and policy publications. He was a 2012–2013 National Review Institute Washington fellow. Dan has testified before the U.S. Congress and several state legislatures on tax and fiscal policy, government reform, and disaster recovery policy.

Rothschild has a bachelor's degree from Grinnell College, a master's degree in modern British history from the University of Manchester, and a master's degree in public policy from the Gerald R. Ford School of Public Policy at the University of Michigan.

RUDD Kevin The Honorable Kevin Rudd AC served as Australia's 26th Prime Minister (2007–2010, 2013) and as Foreign Minister (2010–2012). As Prime Minister, he led Australia's response during the Global Financial Crisis—the only major developed economy not to go into recession—and helped found the G20. While Prime Minister and Foreign Minister, he was active in global and regional foreign policy leadership, and was a driving force in expanding the East Asia Summit to include both the United States and Russia in 2010, and on climate change, he ratified the Kyoto Protocol in 2007.

Mr. Rudd joined the Asia Society Policy Institute as its inaugural President in January 2015. The Institute, headquartered in New York, is a "think- and do-tank" dedicated to tackling major policy challenges confronting the Asia-Pacific in security, prosperity, sustainability, and the development of common norms and values for the region. In 2014, he was named a Senior Fellow with Harvard University's John F. Kennedy School of Government, where he completed a major policy paper on the future of US–China relations under Xi Jinping. From 2015 to 2016 he led a review of the UN system as Chair of the Independent Commission on Multilateralism. He is currently Chair of Sanitation and Water for All and of the International Peace Institute in New York. He is also a Distinguished Fellow at Chatham House and the Paulson Institute, a Distinguished Statesman with the Center for Strategic and International Studies, and a member of the Comprehensive Nuclear Test-Ban Treaty Organization's Group of Eminent Persons. He serves on the International Advisory Board of the Schwarzman Scholars program at Tsinghua University, and is an Honorary Professor at Peking University. Mr. Rudd is proficient in Mandarin Chinese. He also remains actively engaged in indigenous reconciliation.

SALEM Paul Paul Salem is president of The Middle East Institute. He focuses on issues of political change, transition, and conflict as well as the regional and international relations of the Middle East. Salem is the author and editor of a number of books and reports including *Escaping the Conflict Trap: Toward Ending Civil Wars in the Middle East* (ed. with Ross Harrison, MEI 2019); *Winning the Battle, Losing the War: Addressing the Conditions that Fuel Armed Non State Actors* (ed. with Charles Lister, MEI 2019); *From Chaos to Cooperation: Toward Regional*

Order in the Middle East (ed. with Ross Harrison, MEI 2017), *Broken Orders: The Causes and Consequences of the Arab Uprisings* (In Arabic, 2013), "Thinking Arab Futures: Drivers, scenarios, and strategic choices for the Arab World", The Cairo Review Spring 2019; "The Recurring Rise and Fall of Political Islam" (CSIS, 2015), *Bitter Legacy: Ideology and Politics in the Arab World* (1994), and *Conflict Resolution in the Arab World* (ed., 1997). He received his B.A., M.A. and Ph.D. from Harvard University. Prior to joining MEI, Salem was the founding director of the Carnegie Middle East Center in Beirut, Lebanon between 2006 and 2013. From 1999 to 2006, he was director of the Fares Foundation and in 1989–1999 founded and directed the Lebanese Center for Policy Studies, Lebanon's leading public policy think tank.

TANDEN Neera Neera Tanden is the president and CEO of the Center for American Progress and the CEO of the Center for American Progress Action Fund, where she focuses on how both organizations can fulfill their missions to expand opportunity for all Americans. Tanden has also served in both the Obama and Clinton administrations, as well as on presidential campaigns.

Before leading American Progress, Tanden was the organization's chief operating officer. She previously served as senior adviser for health reform at the U.S. Department of Health and Human Services. In that role, she developed policies around reform and worked with Congress and stakeholders on particular provisions of President Barack Obama's signature legislative achievement—the Affordable Care Act.

Prior to that, Tanden was the director of domestic policy for the Obama-Biden presidential campaign, where she managed all domestic policy proposals. Tanden also served as policy director for Hillary Clinton's first presidential campaign, where she directed all policy work and oversaw the debate preparation process for then-Sen. Clinton (D-NY).

Before the 2008 presidential campaign, Tanden served as legislative director in Sen. Clinton's office and deputy campaign manager and issues director for Clinton's 2000 Senate campaign. She began her career as an associate director for domestic policy in former President Bill Clinton's White House and senior policy adviser to the first lady.

Tanden has appeared on NBC's "Meet the Press," ABC's "This Week," CBS' "Face the Nation," PBS' "NewsHour with Jim Lehrer," HBO's "Real Time with Bill Maher," MSNBC, CNN, and Fox. Most recently, she was named to *Elle* magazine's "Women in Washington Power List" and *Politico Magazine*'s "Politico 50," an annual list of the top thinkers, doers, and visionaries in American politics. She has also been included in *National Journal*'s "Washington's Most Influential Women," *Washingtonian* magazine's "Most Powerful Women in Washington," and *Fortune* magazine's "Most Powerful Women in Politics."

Tanden received her Bachelor of Science from the University of California, Los Angeles and her law degree from Yale Law School. She lives in Washington, DC, with her husband and their two children.

VARDI Moshe Y. Moshe Y. Vardi is University Professor and the Karen Ostrum George Distinguished Service Professor of Computational Engineering. He currently leads the Technology, Culture, and Society Initiative at Rice University. He chaired the Computer Science Department at Rice University from 1994 until 2002, and led the Ken Kennedy Institute for Information Technology at Rice University from 2001 until 2019. Prior to joining Rice in 1993, he was at the IBM Almaden Research Center, where he managed the Mathematics and Related Computer Science Department. His research interests include database systems, computational-complexity theory, multi-agent systems, and design specification and verification. Vardi received his Ph.D. from the Hebrew University of Jerusalem in 1981. He is the author and co-author of over 600 articles, as well as two books, "Reasoning about Knowledge" and "Finite Model Theory and Its Applications," and the editor of several collections.

Vardi is the recipient of numerous awards, including three IBM Outstanding Innovation Awards, the 2000 Goedel Prize, the 2005 ACM Kanellakis Award for Theory and Practice, the 2006 LICS Test-of-Time Award, the 2008 ACM PODS Mendelzon Test-of-Time Award, the 2008 ACM SIGMOD Codd Innovations Award, the 2008 Blaise pascal Medal for Computer Science by the European Academy of Sciences, the 2008 ACM Presidential Award, the 2010 CRA Distinguished Service Award, the 2010 ACM Outstanding Contribution Award, the 2011 IEEE Computer Society Harry H. Goode Award, the 2012 EATCS Distinguished Achievements Award, and the Southeastern Universities Research Association's 2013 Distinguished Scientist Award, the 2017 ACM Presidential Award, and the 2018 ACM SIGLOG Church Award. He holds honorary doctorates from the University of Saarland, Germany, the University of Orleans in France, UFRGS in Brazil, the University of Liege in Belgium, the Technical University of Vienna, Austria, and the University of Edinburgh in Scotland, and the University of Grenoble-Alpes. Vardi is an editor of several international journals, and Senior Editor of the Communication of ACM, having served for a decade as Editor-in-Chief. He is Guggenheim Fellow, as well as a Fellow of the American Association for the Advancement of Science, the American Mathematical Society, the Association of Computing Machinery, the Association for the Advancement of Artificial Intelligence, the European Association for Theoretical Computer Science, the Institute for Electrical and Electronic Engineers, and the Society for Industrial and Applied Mathematics. He is a member of the US National Academy of Engineering and National Academy of Science, the American Academy of Arts and Science, the European Academy of Sciences, and the Academia Europaea.

WARTELL Sarah Rosen   In 2012, Sarah Rosen Wartell became the third president of the Urban Institute since it was founded in 1968. Urban is an economic and social science research and policy organization whose more than 450 researchers, experts, and other staff believe in the power of evidence to improve lives and strengthen communities. During her tenure, Urban has articulated its strategy to "elevate the debate" by bringing more of its insights from research to federal, state, and local government and practice; becoming a leader in research communications and data visualization; and undertaking an ambitious program of business systems and technology modernization.

Previously, Wartell was deputy assistant to the president for economic policy and deputy director of the National Economic Council. At the US Department of Housing and Urban Development from 1993 to 1998, she advised the federal housing commissioner on housing finance, mortgage markets, and consumer protection. Later, she was a consultant to the bipartisan Millennial Housing Commission.

After government service, Wartell was the founding chief operating officer and then executive vice president of the Center for American Progress. Before her tenure in government, she practiced law with the Washington, DC, firm Arnold & Porter.

Wartell serves on the board of Enterprise Community Partners and on Bank of America's National Community Advisory Council. She previously served on the boards of the Center for Law and Social Policy, the Low Income Investment Fund, the Center for Urban Science and Progress at New York University, and the Corporation for Enterprise Development. Her areas of expertise include community development, consumer finance, asset building, and housing finance.

Wartell has an AB degree with honors in urban affairs from Princeton University's Woodrow Wilson School of Public and International Affairs. She has a JD degree from Yale Law School.

WEINSTEIN Kenneth R. Dr. Kenneth R. Weinstein serves as President and CEO and Walter P. Stern Chair at Hudson Institute, the Washington-based think tank dedicated to promoting US international leadership and global engagement for a secure, free and prosperous future. Weinstein first joined Hudson in 1991, and worked at numerous think tanks, including The Heritage Foundation, before returning to Hudson in 1999 as Director of the Washington Office, Weinstein, a graduate of The University of Chicago, who earned a graduate degree at Sciences Po (Paris) and a Ph.D. in political philosophy from Harvard University, was promoted to Vice President, COO, CEO and named President and CEO of Hudson Institute in 2011.

Under Weinstein's leadership, the Institute has grown significantly in size, visibility and influence, and has built ties to policymakers around the globe. Weinstein serves as Chairman of the U.S. Agency for Global Media and as a member of the Advisory Committee on Trade Policy and Negotiations, the lead advisory body for the United States Trade Representative. In March 2020, Weinstein was nominated by President Trump to serve as U.S. Ambassador to Japan.

Bibliography

Introduction and Literature Review

Abelson, Donald E. 2000. Do Think Tanks Matter? Opportunities, Constraints and Incentives for Think Tanks in Canada and the United States. *Global Society* 14 (2): 213–236.

Abelson, Donald E. 2006. *A Capitol Idea: Think Tanks and U.S. Foreign Policy.* Montreal: McGill-Queen's University Press.

Ahmad, Mahmood. 2008. US Think Tanks and the Politics of Expertise: Role, Value and Impact. *The Political Quarterly* 79 (4): 529–555.

Bertelli, A., and J. Wenger. 2009. Demanding Information: think Tanks and the US Congress. *British Journal of Political Science* 39 (2): 225–242.

Durst, S., & J. Thurber. 1989. Studying Washington Think Tanks: In Search of Definitions and Data. Paper presented at the Annual Meeting of the American Political Science Association, 31 August–3 September 1989, Atlanta, USA.

Katz, Michael L. 2009. American Think Tanks: Their Influence Is on the Rise. *Carnegie Reporter* 5 (2): 7.

McGann, James G. 1995. *The Competition for Dollars, Scholars, and Influence in the Public Policy Research Industry.* Lanham: University Press of America.

McGann, James G. 2015. *Global Think Tank Innovations Summit Report: The Think Tank of the Future is here Today.* Philadelphia: Think Tanks and Civil Societies Program, University of Pennsylvania.

McGann, James G. 2018. *Think Tanks: A Bridge Over Troubled Waters and Turbulent Times*. Philadelphia: Think Tanks and Civil Societies Program, University of Pennsylvania.

McGann, James G. 2019. *2019 European Think Tanks Summit*. Philadelphia: Think Tanks and Civil Societies Program, University of Pennsylvania.

Orlans, Harold. 1972. *The Nonprofit Research Institute: Its Operation, Origins, Problems, and Prospects*. New York: McGraw-Hill.

Ricci, David M. 1993. *The Transformation of American Politics: The New Washington and the Rise of Think Tanks*. New Haven: Yale University Press.

Stone, Diane. 2000. Think Tanks Transnationalization and Non-Profit Analysis, Advice, and Advocacy. *Global Society* 14 (2): 153–172.

Stone, D. 2013. *Capturing the Political Imagination: Think Tanks and the Policy Process*. London: Routledge.

Weaver, Kent R. 1989. The Changing World of Think Tanks. *Political Science and Politics* 22 (3): 563–578.

Weidenbaum, M. 2010. Measuring the Influence of Think Tanks. *Social Sciences and Public Policy* 47: 134–137.

Wiarda, H.J. 2015. Think Tanks and Foreign Policy in a Globalized World: New Ideas, New "Tanks," New Directions. *International Journal* 70 (4): 517–525.

SUBMISSIONS

Banerjee, Neela. 20 March 2020. Covid-19, Climate Change and Public Health: A Q & A with Aaron Bernstein. The Global Observatory. https://theglobalobservatory.org/2020/03/covid-19-public-health-climate-change-qa-with-aaron-bernstein/#more-20191.

Beavers, Olivia. 5 April 2020. Momentum Grows to Change Medical Supply Chain from China. *The Hill*. https://thehill.com/policy/national-security/491119-momentum-grows-to-change-medical-supply-chain-from-china.

Bell, Ruth Greenspan, and Berry Blechman. 22 December 2012. Global Warming Experts Should Think More About the Cold War. Wilson Center. https://www.wilsoncenter.org/article/global-warming-experts-should-think-more-about-the-cold-war.

Blundell, John. 1987. "How to Move a Nation." Reason.

Boettke, Peter, Emily Chamlee-Wright, Peter Gordon, Sanford Ikeda, Peter Leeson, and Russell Sobel. 2007. The Political, Economic, and Social Aspects of Katrina. *Southern Economic Journal* 74: 363–376.

Califano, Joseph A. 1991. *The Triumph and Tragedy of Lyndon Johnson*. New York: Simon & Schuster Inc.

Center for American Progress. 2019. RELEASE: Medicare Extra Would Provide Universal Coverage and Lower Costs for All for $2.8 Trillion. https://www.americanprogress.org/press/release/2019/07/23/472497/release-medicare-extra-provide-universal-coverage-lower-costs-2-8-trillion/.

Coghlan, David, and Mary Brydon-Miller. 2014. *The Sage Encyclopedia of Action Research*. London, UK: Sage.

Doemeland, Doerte, and James Trevino. 2014. Which World Bank Reports Are Widely Read? (English). Policy Research working paper; no. WPS 6851. Washington, DC: World Bank Group. http://documents.worldbank.org/curated/en/387501468322733597/Which-World-Bank-reports-are-widely-read.

Doffman, Zak. 8 April 2019. Facebook Slammed as 'Morally Bankrupt, Pathological Liars' as Regulation Becomes Real. *Forbes*. https://www.forbes.com/sites/zakdoffman/2019/04/08/facebook-slammed-as-morally-bankrupt-pathological-liars-for-not-acting-on-live-streaming/#17ec0c64200f.

Dorfman, Aaron, and Ellen Dorsey. 19 March 2020. Now Is the Time for Philanthropy to Give More, Not Less. The Chronicle of Philanthropy.

Fennell, Lee Anne. 2011. Ostrom's Law: Property Rights in the Commons. *International Journal of the Commons* 5 (1): 9–27. http://doi.org/10.18352/ijc.252.

Gallup. 2019. Confidence in Institutions. Gallup. https://news.gallup.com/poll/1597/confidence-institutions.aspx.

Glassman, Amanda. 10 March 2020. The Call for a Global Health Security Challenge Fund. Center for Global Development. https://www.cgdev.org/blog/call-global-health-security-challenge-fund.

Hananel, Sam. Center for American Progress. 2019. RELEASE: CAP Issues Framework for 100 Percent Clean Future by 2050. https://www.americanprogress.org/press/release/2019/10/10/475656/release-cap-issues-framework-100-percent-clean-future-2050/.

IPWatchdog. 20 September 2019. Bipartisan Effort to Resurrect Office of Technology Assessment Introduced. https://www.ipwatchdog.com/2019/09/20/bipartisan-effort-resurrect-office-technology-assessment-introduced/id=113584.

Jones, Jeffrey M. 9 October 2018. Confidence in Higher Education Down Since 2015. Gallup. https://news.gallup.com/opinion/gallup/242441/confidence-higher-education-down-2015.aspx.

Kelstrup, Jesper Dahl. 2016. *The Politics of Think Tanks in Europe*. London: Routledge.

King, Meg, and Jake Rosen. 16 July 2019. Building a North American Technology Trust. *Yale Journal of International Affairs*. http://yalejournal.org/article_post/building-a-north-american-technology-trust/.

Levin, Yuval. 2012. "Devaluing the Think Tank." National Affairs.

Mahtani, Shibani. 17 March 2019. Facebook Removed 1.5 Million Videos of the Christchurch Attacks Within 24 Hours—And There Were Still Many More. *The Washington Post*. https://www.washingtonpost.com/world/facebook-removed-15-million-videos-of-the-christchurch-attacks-within-24-hours–and-there-were-still-many-more/2019/03/17/fe3124b2-4898-11e9-b871-978 e5c757325_story.html.

Mangan, Dan. 2017a. 24 Million Would Lose Health Insurance Coverage by 2026 Under GOP's Obamacare Replacement, New Estimate Says. CNBC. https://www.cnbc.com/2017/03/13/cbo-says-millions-lose-health-insurance-under-gop-obamacare-replacement.html.

Mangan, Dan. 2017b. Trump Advisor Conway Says No One Will Lose Health Coverage After Obamacare Repeal. CNBC. https://www.cnbc.com/2017/01/03/trump-adviser-conway-says-no-one-will-lose-health-coverage-after-oba macare-repeal.html.

McIntyre, Lee. 2018. *Post-Truth*. Cambridge, MA: The MIT Press.

Mercatus Center. "Urbanity." Mercatus Center. https://www.mercatus.org/pro grams.

Milanovic, Branko. January/February 2020. The Clash of Capitalisms: The Real Fight for the Global Economy's Future. *Foreign Affairs*.

Murphy, Samantha. 30 April 2014. Facebook Changes Its 'Move Fast and Break Things' Motto. Mashable. https://mashable.com/2014/04/30/facebooks-new-mantra-move-fast-with-stability/.

Noonan, Peggy. 5 October 2017. The Culture of Death—And of Disdain. *The Wall Street Journal*. https://www.wsj.com/articles/the-culture-of-deathand-of-disdain-1507244198.

Okeke, Cameron, and Nancy G. La Vigne. 8 April 2019. Reckoning with Structural Racism in Research: LBJ's Legacy and Urban's Next 50. Urban Institute. https://www.urban.org/urban-wire/reckoning-structural-racism-research-lbjs-legacy-and-urbans-next-50.

Parker, Kim. 19 August 2019. The Growing Partisan Divide in Views of Higher Education. Pew Research Center. https://www.pewsocialtrends.org/essay/the-growing-partisan-divide-in-views-of-higher-education/.

Pew Research Center. 19 September 2019. Why Americans Don't Fully Trust Many Who Hold Positions of Power and Responsibility. Pew Research Center. https://www.people-press.org/2019/09/19/why-americ ans-dont-fully-trust-many-who-hold-positions-of-power-and-responsibility/.

Rauch, Jonathan. 1993. *Kindly Inquisitors: The New Attacks on Free Thought*. Chicago: University of Chicago Press.

Stimson Center. 38 North. https://www.38north.org/.

Szalai, Jennifer. 12 December 2018. A Look at Competition in Business Urges Us to Think Small. *The New York Times*. https://www.nytimes.com/2018/12/12/books/review-curse-of-bigness-antitrust-law-tim-wu.html.

Urban Institute. Next 50. https://next50.urban.org/.

Vick, Karl. 24 December 2018, & 31 December 2018. Person of the Year 2018. *Time*. https://time.com/person-of-the-year-2018-the-guardians/.

Zenko, Micah. 14 July 2011. City of Men. *Foreign Policy*. https://foreignpolicy.com/2011/07/14/city-of-men/.

Zuckerman, Ethan. 14 August 2014. The Internet's Original Sin. *The Atlantic*. https://www.theatlantic.com/technology/archive/2014/08/advertising-is-the-internets-original-sin/376041/.

Conclusion

Avins, Jeremy. 25 November 2013. Strategy Is a Fundraising Necessity, Not a Luxury. *On Think Tanks*. Accessed 7 November 2018. https://onthinktanks.org/articles/strategy-is-afundraising-necessity-not-a-luxury/.

Bennett, Amanda. 5 October 2015. Are Think Tanks Obsolete? *The Washington Post*. Accessed 7 November 2018. https://www.washingtonpost.com/news/in-theory/wp/2015/10/05/are-think-tanksobsolete/?noredirect=on&utm_ter&utm_term=.20802394eb95.

Henke, Nicolaus, Jacques Bughin, Michael Chui, James Manyika, Tamim Saleh, Bill Wiseman, and Guru Sethupathy. December 2016. The Age of Analytics: Competing in a Data-driven World. McKinsey Global Institute. Accessed 6 November 2018. https://www.mckinsey.com/business-functions/mckinsey-analytics/our-insights/theage-of-analytics-competing-in-a-data-driven-world.

Kuntz, Fred. 11 July 2013.Communications and Impact Metrics for Think Tanks. Centre for International Governance Innovation. Accessed 7 November 2018. http://www.cigionline.org/articles/communications-and-impact-metrics-think-tanks.

Lipton, Eric, and Brooke Williams. 20 January 2018. How Think Tanks Amplify Corporate America's Influence. *The New York Times*. Accessed 7 November 2018. http://www.nytimes.com/2016/08/08/us/politics/think-tanks-research-andcorporate-lobby.

McGann, James G. 9 February 2016. 2015 Global Go to Think Tank Index Report. Scholarly Commons, University of Pennsylvania. Accessed November 7, 2018. https://repository.upenn.edu/think_tanks/10/.

Numanović, Amar. 11 July 2017. Data Science: The Next Frontier for Data-Driven Policy Making? Medium. Accessed 7 November 2018. https://medium.com/@numanovicamar/https-medium-com-numanovicamar-datascience-the-next-frontier-for-data-driven-policy-making-8abe98159748.

Ovans, Andrea. 6 December 2017. What Is a Business Model? *Harvard Business Review*. Accessed 7 November 2018. https://hbr.org/2015/01/what-is-a-business-model.

Ralphs, Gerard. 14 June 2016. Think Tank Business Models: The Business of Academia and Politics. *On Think Tanks*. Accessed 7 November 2018. https://onthinktanks.org/articles/think-tank-business-models-the-business-ofacademia-and-politics/.

Zhu, Xufeng. 23 June 2017. A New Ranking: The 2016 Big Data Report on Chinese Think Tanks. *On Think Tanks*. Accessed 7 November 2018. https://onthinktanks.org/resources/a-new-ranking-the-2016-big-data-report-onchinese-think-tanks/.

The manufacturer's authorised representative in the EU is Springer Nature Customer Service Centre GmbH, Europaplatz 3, 69115 Heidelberg, Germany. If you have any concerns regarding our products, please contact ProductSafety@springernature.com

Printed and bound by CPI Group (UK) Ltd, Croydon, CR0 4YY
05/05/2026
02102750-0001